You Can Have As Far As You Can See

You Can Have As Far As You Can See

Dr. F. Bruce Williams

Copyright © 2012 Dr. F. Bruce Williams

Scripture quotations are taken from the Holy Bible, King James Version, Cambridge, 1769. (Public Domain).

DEDICATION:

To those who are ready to embark on a new journey, to chart undiscovered territory, to tread on the land as far as they can see.

ACKNOWLEDGEMENTS

First and foremost I want to thank God for choosing me to serve and for giving me a passion to show the "least of these" that there is greatness in all of us.

My wonderful wife, Michelle, who has been a constant source of support and encouragement to me, unselfishly providing me the time and sacred space at home to pray, think, plan, work and write. I could not have done this without her, my partner, lover and friend.

My beautiful children, Imani and Nailah.

I want to thank the wonderful and dedicated staff and members of Bates Memorial Baptist Church for believing in me and giving me the space to stretch myself and use all of my gifts to be a blessing to others for the sake of the Kingdom.

May the Lord bless you all for helping to make this book a reality.

~Dr. F. Bruce Williams

TABLE OF CONTENTS

INTRODUCTION	7
YOU CAN HAVE AS FAR AS YOU CAN SEE	11
MOM, I OWE YOU	17
FATHERS, THE FAMILY AND HOW TO MAKE A COMEBACK	29
REFLECTIONS ON 9/11	37
ONE MORE VOICE	41
DON'T FALL ASLEEP	46
HONORING 'THE CALL'	81
A REMEDY FOR A SNAKE BITE	90
THANK YOU LORD	110
THE GREATEST GIFT OF ALL	126
HOW TO HAVE GOOD SUCCESS	140

INTRODUCTION

You Can Have As Far As You Can See contains a combination of full length sermons, medium length reflections and brief musings on various topics. It is designed to stir the imagination, stimulate faith and inspire hope in the human heart. The title for this book is taken from the first piece that appears in this collection of works. While this book was not written as one work, per se, this collection of works shares a common theme - hope. It can be read straight through or it can be read randomly, with the reader choosing to read a chapter according to the title or topic that interests the reader at any given time.

Chapter One begins with a call to claim your inheritance in God by realizing that, "You Can Have As Far As You Can See". It seeks to stimulate hope in the heart so that one can dream big and walk by faith claiming the promises of God. Chapter Two, "Mom, I Owe You", is a Mother's Day reflection in the form of a 'thank you' to my mother. It's designed to give hope to struggling mothers by gleaning from the life of Jochebed, the mother of Moses, powerful principles for successfully raising children in an environment that is often hostile and dangerous. Chapter Three, entitled, "Fathers, the Family and How to Make a Comeback", is words of hope to fathers' declaring that no matter how hopeless your home situation may seem, you can, with the help of the Lord, start to reclaim your family and start all over again. Chapter Four is musings on 9/11 inspired by the tenth anniversary of that tragic event. It, too, is a word of hope for the heart insisting that we can heal and triumph beyond the horror of that day. Chapter Five is a reference to the Occupy Movement entitled, "One More Voice". It is a brief piece where I add my voice to the chorus of voices that rise up in righteous indignation against injustice caused by greed and avarice. The very fact that voices rise is evidence that even in the face of injustice there are those who have a vision of hope for a better day. Chapter Six, "Don't Fall Asleep", is a sermonic warning to the 'sleeping' and a call to remain awake because those who remain truly awake are those who have hope and inspire hope for the suffering. Chapter Seven entitled, "Honoring the Call", is my reflection on keeping the integrity of the divine call to preach. Unfortunately, many who claim to be called, dishonor the call and undermine hope because they are looking at what they can gain rather than seeing how they can give. Chapter Eight, "A Remedy for Snake Bite", shares with the reader the hope of how to handle the inevitable attack of poisonous people and painful predicaments. Chapter Nine, "Thank You Lord", was inspired by the Thanksgiving Season. It's a word about gratitude and how an attitude of gratitude helps one see God and life in a way that inspires hope and praise and stimulates one to recommitment oneself to God afresh. Chapter Ten, "The Greatest Gift of All", was inspired by the Christmas season celebrating the arrival of the true source of all hope, Jesus the Christ! Finally, Chapter Eleven, "How to Have Good Success", offers hope for those who seek to live a successful life by redefining what true success is and offering guidance to realize God's *good* success!

The life we have is gift from God. I believe God intends for us to make the most of it, to live it to the fullest, to dream big, to accomplish great things and above all, to serve others. As you seek to live the life that God has ordained for you, keep your hand in God's hand, keep your feet in God's will, keep God's love in your heart, keep your eyes on the horizon, and have the audacity to believe that you can have as far as you can see!

YOU CAN HAVE AS FAR AS YOU CAN SEE

Genesis 13:15-17

15For all the land which thou seest, to thee will I give it, and to thy seed for ever. 16And I will make thy seed as the dust of the earth: so that if a man can number the dust of the earth, then shall thy seed also be numbered.17Arise, walk through the land in the length of it and in the breadth of it; for I will give it unto thee.

In our text God invites Abraham to walk on the land that he had promised him. But before he tells him to walk on the land, in verse 15 he says something else to him. Before he tells him to use his feet, he tells him to use his eyes. He says in Genesis 13:15: "All the land which you can see, to you will I give it..." In other words, "all the land you can see, you can have." Another way of saying that is, "You can have as far as you can see." What a powerful promise. "You can have as far as you can see." If you can see it, you can have it.

The exciting thing about this promise is that the same is true for you and me today. We too can have as far as we can see. I am not talking about seeing with the eyes in our head, but with the eyes of our minds. I don't mean seeing with our physical eyes, I mean seeing with the eyes of our sanctified imagination. I am not referring to physical eyesight; I am referring to spiritual insight. That is called vision; being able to see what God has for you to possess and to accomplish. That is why part of our daily prayers ought to be that the Lord would open our eyes and let us see the expanse of his blessings in our lives. Ask God to give you a vision of what is possible for you in him.

What you can see is important because you can only have what you are able to see. If you can't see it, you can't have it. And if you can't see much, then you can't have much. If you can only see a little, then you can only have a little. What you can have is limited only by what you can see. Haven't you ever heard people say "I just can't see it"? Well, as long as they can't see it they won't have it. They will never be able to achieve in their lives what they cannot conceive in their minds. What can you see? Whatever you can conccive you can achieve. It doesn't matter how great God's plans are for your life, if you can't see them, then you will never have them. But if you dare to dream, if you stretch your mind, if you expand your imagination, if you can just look a little farther than you are used to looking, if you can see for you what God has in store for you, then you can have as far as you can see. It starts with vision.

This principle is something we have to teach to our children. If we want to help our children to become great achievers, if we want to prepare our young ones to do great things with their lives, then we've got to teach them to have vision. We have to take the shackles of limitation off of their small, developing minds and let them know that when it comes to their personal achievement the sky is the limit. We have to stop telling them that they will never be able to achieve because of racism, poverty, oppression or a host of other obstacles that certainly stand in their way. When we do that we are not teaching them to succeed, we are teaching them to fail. We have got to teach them that God has great aspirations for their lives. And then we must teach them to dream so big and broad that when negative forces conspire to limit them, they don't see them as problems to resign to, but they see them as obstacles to overcome. When they ask us, what can I achieve with my life, we have to teach them that, in the Lord, they can have as far as they can see.

The problem with many of us is that we have limited vision. Our lives are mediocre because our vision is mediocre. Since what we dare to see is so limited, it affects every other aspect of our lives. Our limited vision produces limited living. We are still stuck in the same old unsatisfying life, because we just can't see how it can get any better. Our marriages are mediocre because our vision for our marriages is mediocre. We can't have any better because we can't see any better. We are still hooked on the same old habits because we can't see how we can overcome. We are still stuck with same old boyfriend or girlfriend in the same old sick, destructive relationship because we can't see ourselves living without him or her. We are still stuck in the same old dead-end job because we just can't see ourselves getting a better one. We are still bogged down in the same old financial mess because we just can't see how we can ever get out. We are still haunted and frustrated by the fact that we still have not started that business we have always wanted to start because we just can't see how it can happen for us. We have given up on that dream to go to school and earn a degree, learn a skill, take a course or improve ourselves all because we just can't see how we can ever do it. Well, if you can't see it, you can't have it. But whatever you can see you can have!

Can you see yourself with a degree? Keep that thought because it's yours. Can you see yourself with a better marriage? Keep that thought because it's yours. Can you see yourself with that career you've always wanted? Can you see yourself with better financial stability? Hold those thoughts because it's all yours. Can you see yourself with better character, stronger faith, a sweeter spirit, better patience or deeper love? Hold that thought, keep that concept, believe that vision, and claim that inheritance, because you can have as far as you can see!

MOM, I OWE YOU

Exodus 2:1-10

1And there went a man of the house of Levi, and took to wife a daughter of Levi. 2And the woman conceived, and bare a son: and when she saw him that he was a goodly child, she hid him three months. 3And when she could not longer hide him, she took for him an ark of bulrushes, and daubed it with slime and with pitch, and put the child therein; and she laid it in the flags by the river's brink. 4And his sister stood afar off, to wit what would be done to him. 5And the daughter of Pharaoh came down to wash herself at the river; and her maidens walked along by the river's side; and when she saw the ark among the flags, she sent her maid to fetch it. 6And when she had opened it, she saw the child: and, behold, the babe wept. And she had compassion on him, and said, This is one of the Hebrews' children. 7Then said his sister to Pharaoh's daughter, Shall I go and call to thee a nurse of the Hebrew women, that she may nurse the child for thee?

8And Pharaoh's daughter said to her, Go. And the maid went and called the child's mother. 9And Pharaoh's daughter said unto her, Take this child away, and nurse it for me, and I will give thee thy wages. And the women took the child, and nursed it.

10And the child grew, and she brought him unto Pharaoh's daughter, and he became her son. And she called his name Moses: and she said, Because I drew him out of the water.

May is the month for Mothers Day! When I think of my mother I am reminded, among other things, that I owe my mother so very much. From the moment I was conceived in my mother's womb, a combination of her biology and her love nourished and nurtured my life. In her womb was where I began developing as a baby boy. In her womb I took my first breath, sustained by the oxygenated blood that flowed through her veins. Her womb was my first dormitory, my first living quarters, a shelter from the blasts of life. Her womb was my first cafeteria, where I received my first meals, connected to her by an umbilical cord so that whatever she ate I ate. Her womb was my first cradle, there suspended in amniotic fluid, whenever I got tired, the movement of my mother rocked me to sleep. I owe my mother so much.

And then that big day came. Finally I left her womb to make my debut on the stage of human history! But my birth did not come without great cost to my mother. The birth process is excruciating and almost unbearable. Mothers die a little bringing us into the world. But maternal instinct and motherly love is so strong that even though the birth is painful, the pain of the birth is swallowed up in the love of the mother for her child; and the joy that her child has safely arrived. Even before the first bottle was made, diaper changed, bath given or wound healed; I automatically owed a great debt to my mother.

Then my mother began the awesome task of rearing me as a young boy. Fortunately, she had the help of my wonderful father, but my mother was an incredible mother for me. Now that I am an adult and a parent, I realize it is not easy being a mother and raising children. I believe that it was particularly difficult for her trying to raise a Black boy in our society. I was born in 1959, so I imagine that it had to be a struggle raising an African American child in the cultural climate of that time. The fact is, Black and Brown people still have to struggle against the tide of injustice and racism, both personal and institutional. We still live in a time when Black and Brown males are disproportionately stopped, searched, arrested, convicted and incarcerated by our criminal justice system. Black and Brown boys and girls are still a part of the population that falls disproportionately below the poverty line; Black and Brown boys are still disproportionately dropping out of schools at alarming rates. Black boys who grow up to be Black men still have a shorter life span than their White counterparts. Stress, inequality, oppression, racism, poverty all conspire to create an environment that makes it difficult to raise a child. But even against those odds, my mother did it! I owe my mother so much.

With my mother being a Christian, I am sure that my mom was also concerned about raising me amid the moral temptations of our time. Her desire was that her children live according to the will of God and not be adversely influenced by the immoral and unethical forces around us. There were then and there are now, moral and cultural forces vying for the attention and allegiance of our children. Everywhere you turn, there seems to be some morally twisted and distorted influence seeking to bruise, shatter and even demean the hearts, minds, spirits and self esteem of our children. It's hard raising children in an environment like that!

But being a strong Black woman of faith and fortitude, my mother was diligent about our upbringing. Now, she was not stiff, stuffy, stilted, harsh, narrow, or cold in her efforts either. She was and is the kind of woman who loves to drink deeply from life. So she showed us that living by Christian principles does not have to make life dull and depressing but instead makes life vibrant and alive! We were taught that living for the Lord with a sense of moral and ethical integrity added to life and did not take away from life. We learned this under her capable direction. And I owe her for that.

How did she do it? When I consider that question, I am reminded of how Jochebed raised Moses amid similar circumstances. Jochebed raised her child during Egyptian slavery. She raised her child, Moses, in a dangerous, deadly and depressing environment full of stress, oppression, male targeted infanticide and moral challenges. But she did it! In fact, her son turned out to be the liberator of an entire nation. And while I do not claim to be a liberator like Moses, I do realize that my mother successfully raised me (and my siblings) in similar circumstances, against great odds. And, you know, we didn't turn out too bad!

When I thought about it, I realized that my mother raised us using the same principles Jochebed used to raise Moses. First, my mother isolated us. Exodus 2:2 says the following about the strategy

Jochebed used while Moses was a baby,: "she hid him". That's called isolation.

There were things that conspired to take her baby boy out when he was young, weak, impressionable and vulnerable so the Bible says "she hid him." She understood that he was not yet equipped to deal with many of the things that life had in store for him yet, so she hid him. She did her best to isolate her child from anything that would hurt him in mind, body or spirit. Life was so rough, and he was so young, weak and vulnerable that she decided to control what her child was exposed to, for his own good.

When I think back over my life it occurs to me that my mother did the same thing. Early in my life, while I was still developing, exploring, soaking up the stimuli around me, my mother recognized that it was too early for me to be exposed to certain things. When my mother was raising my siblings and me, while we were real young, she realized that we did not have the strength of character, psychological capacity nor spiritual wherewithal to handle certain sights, sounds, circumstances and even relationships. There were certain foods we couldn't eat, drinks we couldn't drink, places we couldn't go, behaviors we couldn't witness, things we couldn't read, movies we didn't see, television shows we couldn't watch, conversations we could not hear, ways we couldn't dress and even people we couldn't be around. She did this because my mother understood that it is possible to expose small minds and hearts to things way too soon! And I owe her for that.

She not only isolated me for life, my mother insulated me for life. When Jochebed could no longer hide her baby she made a little boat and she lined it was a substance on the inside of it to insulate it against the Nile River. She then put her son in the little ark and set the ark on Nile River. But because of what she put inside the ark, it was able to stay afloat by keeping what was outside of the ark, the Nile, from leaking in and causing it to sink and thereby causing her son to drown. This was during a time when the Pharaoh was having baby boys thrown into the Nile River and drowned. But because of what Jochebed did for the Ark, her son Moses was floating on what other children were drowning in.

My mother helped me stay afloat on the Nile of life by insulating me. She did for me what Jochebed did for that ark. She put something in that was designed to resist the negative forces outside of me that conspired to cause me to sink and drown. She taught me values and principles that keep me afloat in deep and sometimes dangerous waters in life. She gave me a God consciousness and taught me that there is a powerful and loving God with whom I can have a personal relationship and that he is my Lord and loving leader in life. She taught me that I am never alone. She taught me a powerful work ethic too. "Don't be lazy," she said. There is no substitute for hard work! She taught me that it's always right to do right. She taught me the love ethic of Jesus. She taught me to respect women. She taught me to love and respect myself. She taught me to value my culture and celebrate my blackness. She taught me the value of education. Education is something that nothing or no one can take away from you. She taught me to live by faith and not be controlled by fear. And she taught me to keep on growing. My mother made me believe that I could succeed. And she taught me so much more. She insulated me emotionally, psychologically, intellectually, socially and spiritually. The lessons and principles that my mother taught me have kept me afloat while so many of my friends, who lived by different principles, ended up sinking. I owe my mother for that.

Once Jochebed put Moses in the little ark, she released him on the Nile River. In a real sense, that is what my mother did. Once she isolated and insulated me, she was then inspired to release me and set me afloat on the river of life. She did the best she could in raising me but then when I was ready, she released me. I left home. However, she released me because she trusted that God would take care of me. She trusted God and she taught me to do the same. My life has had its share of good times and bad. But in the midst of it all, because of God and my mother, I have a wonderful family and a blessed life. So, I owe my mother so much. I can never repay my mom for what she has done, but she doesn't expect me to. She would probably tell me that the best way to pay her back is make the most of my life! So Mama, I'm going to pay you what I owe you by making you proud of me and making sure that I don't waste this life that you and God gave me. At the very least, that is what I owe!

FATHERS, THE FAMILY AND HOW TO MAKE A COMEBACK
1 Samuel 30:3-19

3So David and his men came to the city, and, behold, it was burned with fire; and their wives, and their sons, and their daughters, were taken captives. 4Then David and the people that were with him lifted up their voice and wept, until they had no more power to weep. 5And David's two wives were taken captives, Ahinoam the Jezreelitess, and Abigail the wife of Nabal the Carmelite.

6And David was greatly distressed; for the people spake of stoning him, because the soul of all the people was grieved, every man for his sons and for his daughters: but David encouraged himself in the LORD his God. 7And David said to Abiathar the priest, Ahimelech's son, I pray thee, bring me hither the ephod. And Abiathar brought thither the ephod to David. 8And David enquired at the LORD, saying, Shall I pursue after this troop? shall I overtake them? And he answered him, Pursue: for thou shalt surely overtake them, and without fail recover all. 9So David went, he and the six hundred men that were with him, and came to the brook Besor, where those that were left behind stayed.

10But David pursued, he and four hundred men: for two hundred abode behind, which were so faint that they could not go over the brook Besor. 11And they found an Egyptian in the field, and brought him to David, and gave him bread, and he did eat; and they made him drink water; 12And they gave him a piece of a cake of figs, and two clusters of raisins: and when he had eaten, his spirit came again to him: for he had eaten no bread, nor drunk any water, three days and three nights. 13And David said unto him, To whom belongest thou? and whence art thou? And he said, I am a young man of Egypt, servant to an Amalekite; and my master left me, because three days agone I fell sick. 14We made an invasion upon the south of the Cherethites, and upon the coast which belongeth to Judah, and upon the south of Caleb; and we burned Ziklag with fire. 15And David said to him, Canst thou bring me down to this company? And he said, Swear unto me by God, that thou wilt neither kill me, nor deliver me into the hands of my master, and I will bring thee down to this company. 16And when he had brought him down, behold, they were spread abroad upon all the earth, eating and drinking, and dancing, because of all the great spoil that they had taken out of the land of the Philistines, and out of the land of Judah.

17And David smote them from the twilight even unto the evening of the next day: and there escaped not a man of them, save four hundred young men, which rode upon camels, and fled. 18And David recovered all that the Amalekites had carried away: and David rescued his two wives. 19And there was nothing lacking to them, neither small nor great, neither sons nor daughters, neither spoil, nor any thing that they had taken to them: David recovered all.

What is often at the forefront of any discussion about the Black family is the issue of fathers and fatherhood. We have heard the staggering statistical data as it relates to single parent households headed by mothers, Black men in prison, dead beat dads, absentee fathers and a host of other ills. We must be dedicated and diligent in dealing with dads because our families, children and therefore our future are at stake.

However, one of the things of late that has been encouraging to me in ministry is the increasing number of black men who are trying to make a comeback regarding their status and responsibilities as fathers. We often hear sermons and lessons talking about how bad fathers are and there are often scores of lessons that are designed to help fathers who are already being good dads become even better dads. But what about those who have been on the sidelines; who have fallen by the wayside and now want to try to get back into the race? Is it too late? I don't believe it is. So for all the fathers who are trying to make a comeback, this one's for you!

The text of scriptures chosen is not technically about fathers and fatherhood but it has housed within it principles that are designed to empower fathers who are trying to make a comeback. The text reports an episode in the life of King David. The incident happened before David took the throne as King. While David was on the run from King Saul he had gathered a group of men around him and was giving leadership to this group of men. At the time, their base of operation was at a place called Ziklag, the place where their families were encamped. Once, while David and the fathers were out busy doing the things that they believed would help provide for their families, they returned and discovered that the enemy had come and kidnapped their families. They were so grieved at such a precious loss that they began to weep until they no longer had strength or tears left.

Soon, their grief turned to anger and they were so furious that they began to blame David for their dire circumstances. In fact, the text says that they were so angry that they were talking about stoning David to death. At this point the story could have taken the worse turn possible. They could have carried out their plan to kill their leader and lost their families forever. Instead, the men do not kill David and in the end the men and David end up rescuing their families from the hands of the enemy. I maintain that the story has housed within it lessons that can help fathers make a comeback. I want to share these brief points and hopefully they will arm fathers with sound advice to reclaim our families.

If we are going to reclaim our families we must first face the problem (verse 3). When David and the men returned they saw their homes destroyed and their families stolen. There was no way of denying what they had lost. If we are going to recover our families and fatherhood then we have to come out of denial and face the problem. Why? Because you and God can't fix what you won't face. If we are going to make a comeback then we have got to be man enough to take responsibility. No matter how bad things look, if you will take "response-ability" then, God will give you the ability to respond.

Go ahead and grieve (verse 4). David and the men cried until they could cry no more. Some people say that wet cheeks on a man are a badge of shame. I disagree. The fact that we have lost our families must matter to us. Our families must matter to us. Our hearts have to be broken before our families can be restored. The reason why some of us are not recovering our families is because we don't care. Or if we do, we have to act like we don't. But let's quit fronting! If you are hurting because you have lost your family and you want your family back, go ahead and acknowledge it. Go ahead and feel the pain of it. Go ahead and grieve over the loss.

Third, take action. There comes a time when the weeping and wailing must cease and we must take action! David and the men went to take back what the enemy stole. When I look at the text I believe I see a plan. Here is the action plan:

•Be encouraged. (verse 6) Don't spend a lot of time playing the blame game.

•Talk to the Lord. (verse 8) The Bible says that David inquired of the Lord. David got the ephod to get a word from the Lord. And God told him what to do. Prayer can do that. Prayer mixed with the word can do that.

•Partner with other fathers .(verse 9) David and his men went together. Find fathers who are serious about being real fathers. Restoring families and raising children will take the combined efforts of fathers working together. If we work together we can reclaim and strengthen our families and children.

•Don't give up! (verses 9-10) Develop some stamina. Remember that whether you are starting out as a new father or you are in a fight for restoration to be the father you should have been, sometimes fatherhood is a fight and the journey can be hard. Recovery will not come without effort. Lazy fathers don't stand a chance. You've got to learn to be faithful even when you don't feel like it. You come home and you are exhausted but your son or daughter needs your attention. Don't faint. Don't make excuses. Perhaps you will need a moment to catch your breath, but don't falter or fall, suck it up and give them the attention they need. You may be involved in some baby mama drama. I know that it gets rough and you want to just give up and explain to the child later, when they are grown why you made a decision to forfeit involvement in their lives. But you will regret it in the end. Do what it takes to work things out. Be in your child's life as best you can no matter how hectic things get. They would rather hear how you fought to be in their lives rather than why you gave up the fight! Besides, the text teaches us that if you keep going God has a way of providing you unexpected assistance along the way. (verses 11-16) The Bible says while they were on the journey to restoring their families they ran into an Egyptian who helped them find their families. There is no quick fix. The scriptures report that David and his men had to fight from dusk until evening the next day. But, the fight will be worth the reward. David and the men recovered all they lost! Praise the Lord!!! God is able to help you restore what was lost. And when that happens there will be joy unspeakable!

REFLECTIONS ON 9/11

On September 11, 2001 terrorists flying jet liners slammed into the Twin Towers of the World Trade Center in New York City, the Pentagon and a field in Shanksville, Pennsylvania. That tragic event changed the lives of millions of people and indeed, changed this nation. It happened more than 10 years ago, but for so many, both the memory and the wounds are still fresh, as if it happened only yesterday.

I am certain that there are as many memories of that day as there are people. I remember the horror of that day. I remember thinking, "Is this really happening?" I remember the towers belching thick clouds of black smoke after being hit by the jet liners. I remember the awful images of desperate people leaping from the towers. I remember people on the ground watching in panic stricken disbelief. I remember both citizens and police trying to get people to safety. I remember people running and the towers finally collapsing. I remember the feelings of utter shock, disbelief and helplessness I felt. I remember wondering if friends of mine were safe in the midst of the chaos. I remember the heavy clouds of dust from the fallen buildings and hearing the screams of horror. I remember people emerging from the rubble, covered in the dust. I remember wondering, "What are we going to do now?" I remember.

One image that stays stuck in my mind from that day, is the image of people emerging from the dust of the collapsed buildings. I saw people arm in arm. I saw people helping to carry one another. I saw people, some total strangers no doubt, huddled together, leaning on one another, helping one another move from the dust to safety. Everyone was covered in dust and I couldn't tell who was who. I couldn't tell who was black, brown, yellow or white. I couldn't tell who was white collar or blue collar. I couldn't tell who was male or female. I couldn't tell who was Democrat or Republican. I couldn't tell who practiced what faith or whether they ascribed to any faith at all. I just saw desperate, hurting people helping one another through a tragic time. For once, what mattered most, was the commonality of our humanity. For once, we Americans seemed to realize in the midst of tragedy, that despite all of our differences, one thing is for certain - we all shiver in the cold, we all sweat in the heat, and if you cut us, we all bleed red blood. Those coming through the smoke made it to safety by helping one another; by working together.

So many things have happened since that awful moment. Inevitably we have to continue to face the task of moving forward in the face of such tragedies. To live on. To rebuild. To heal. How do you do that? It can be done. It's not easy. But it's necessary. If we are to do it well, we have to do it together. Dr. Martin Luther King, Jr. was correct when he declared, "we are all caught up in an inescapable web of mutuality and tied in a single garment of destiny." We need one another. We cannot make the tragic mistake of painting all

Muslims with the same paint brush. I am convinced that those who were guilty of committing the tragic murder of American citizens on 9/11 in 2001 do not represent the attitude of the vast majority of Muslims. Their actions were not ultimately motivated by faith in God. They used God and the cloak of religiosity to justify actions fueled by bitterness and hatred. So we cannot, ten years later or any amount of time, let the actions of a few make us suspicious of all.

    I will never forget the image of those persons emerging from the dust of the collapsed twin towers. In a real sense, more than ten years later, we are still emerging from that dust. We are still trying to get our footing, still trying to survive the tragedy; still trying to figure out how to go on. How do we do it? How do we go on? The same way those covered with the dust of tragedy did then: together.

ONE MORE VOICE

Matthew 25:40

And the King shall answer and say unto them, Verily I say unto you, Inasmuch as ye have done it unto one of the least of these my brethren, ye have done it unto me.

There is an interesting and insightful phenomenon taking place in our country right now. It is being called Occupy Wall Street or OWS. Countless people are showing their utter discontent with our electorate regarding the way our economy is being handled. Actually, what so many of them are insisting is that they are tired of not being heard. Scores of protestors are claiming that our elected officials are paying attention to the money of special interest groups rather than the concerns voiced by the common citizen. They feel ignored and indeed belittled by "the powers that be."

One of things that make this so crucial is that the average citizen is suffering because corporate greed, among other things, has brought our economy to its knees and there seems to be little or no accountability. The average citizen is left to suffer from the result of avarice out of control. Then to add insult to injury, no one seems to be listening to the sufferers. It seems like no one cares.

The electorate could have just rolled over and played dead or they could have simply succumbed to feelings of hopelessness, frustration and despair. But instead, they got angry and decided that enough is enough. Since no one seemed to be paying attention to them, they decided to get people's attention. Thus, Occupy Wall Street. And now, all over the country, people are occupying public spaces in various places to dramatize the frustration citizens feel about the state of our country and the attitude of our national leadership.

This grassroots movement is inspirational. There are those who have tried to minimize the movement by suggesting that it is nothing more than a group of directionless troublemakers with no real rhyme or reason to their actions. Others have suggested that their actions are senseless, that instead of occupying space they should be engaging in meaningful dialogue in ways that produce solutions to the problems they are complaining about. I was watching a group of people on TV make this claim. The interesting thing was that it never dawned on the people who made this complaint that the reason they were sitting down having the discussion on TV in the first place was because of the people who were engaged in the "occupy" movement!

I, for one, am impressed by the actions of those occupiers. For me, what we see is the actions of those who once felt powerless and voiceless finding a creative way to use their power and voice to steer public conversation, debate and discussion in the direction that it should have been headed all along.

The movement seems to be growing. One of the characteristics and perhaps strengths of the movement is its diversity. There are young people and seniors, anarchists and conservatives, employed and unemployed, Democrats and Republicans, military and civilian, working and retired, poor, middle class and upper middle class, famous and infamous, black white, yellow and brown, who are engaged in or lending their support to the movement. This has to do, I think, in large measure, to the fact that the present state of the economy has affected every kind of person of almost every strata of our society. The struggling economy has created common ground. We are the 99%.

As a Christian, I am compelled to voice my support of the movement because it contains the voice of the poor and oppressed. I am compelled to say "amen" to the basic spirit of what is taking place because it involves issues of justice. As a follower of Jesus, I feel affinity to those who protest because their voices contain the voices of "the least of these." Greed, avarice, apathy, indifference, political bribery and abuse of power have conspired to create the conditions that have inspired a grassroots frustration that has emboldened masses of people to speak up and demand that something be done.

A change is coming. With each passing day more people find something in the movement that resonates within them. The times are hard. The future is uncertain. People are frustrated and no longer trust that politicians remember why they have been given power by the electorate. The power has not been given to pad politicians' pockets nor serve the politicians personal or political interest. They were given the power by the people to serve the interest of the people and to do what is in the best interest of this nation. A change is coming. The masses are speaking. Today, I add my voice to theirs.

Don't Fall Asleep

Acts 20:7-12

7And upon the first day of the week, when the disciples came together to break bread, Paul preached unto them, ready to depart on the morrow; and continued his speech until midnight. 8And there were many lights in the upper chamber, where they were gathered together. 9And there sat in a window a certain young man named Eutychus, being fallen into a deep sleep: and as Paul was long preaching, he sunk down with sleep, and fell down from the third loft, and was taken up dead. 10And Paul went down, and fell on him, and embracing him said, Trouble not yourselves; for his life is in him. 11When he therefore was come up again, and had broken bread, and eaten, and talked a long while, even till break of day, so he departed. 12And they brought the young man alive, and were not a little comforted.

We have here housed in this text a simple story of a young boy who falls asleep during the worship service. I was captivated by this story because when you think of all of the material that Luke penned regarding the missionary journeys of Paul, it seems kind of strange that Luke would take pen to paper and pen a seemingly innocuous story about a young boy who falls asleep in church. After all, Luke had witnessed and recorded God doing some miraculous things in the life and ministry of the Apostle Paul. Luke had recorded extraordinary, life changing, hair raising, city transforming situations where people were miraculously healed, souls were saved, churches were established and riots were stirred where Paul was arrested, beaten or stoned or where Paul escaped life threatening situations by the skin of his teeth. And in midst of all of that, Luke chooses to record seemingly superfluous information about a boy who falls asleep in church.

I am convinced that the information is not as insignificant as it may seem. If we would look at this information with closer investigation we can not only discover practical principles that will enhance our own worship experience but we can also learn lessons that can help us live better lives after the benediction.

Come with me if you will to the city of Troas. Paul has stopped there on his way to the Holy city of Jerusalem. While there, he is no doubt developing new relationships with people and they are in turn discovering what a great Christian man and Apostle he is. In fact, I am certain that even before Paul arrived in Troas his reputation had preceded him. So, when he stopped in Troas there were already people there who knew the kind and caliber of person he was.

As he moved among them it soon became evident that it would not be long before Paul would have to leave. As each day passed they knew he was coming closer to his last day there. As that day approached someone must have suggested that given the kind of person Paul was and the kind of things he knew, it would be appropriate, before he left, to hear a last word from him, perhaps a last sermon. So that's apparently what they do. They organize an opportunity for believers to come from far and wide so that they could hear the last words of a great man. And you can imagine that the Christian community made a concerted effort to be there because you should always pay attention to the last words of a great man.

They decided to meet in a room, on the third floor of a borrowed house. The text tells us when they met. They met on the first day of the week. This information is an indication that the New Testament church shifted from meeting on Saturday (the Sabbath) to meeting on Sunday, the first day of the week. It's understandable that the church would make Sunday the day that they began to meet because Sunday was the day that death died. It was the day that Jesus, the conquering hero of Calvary, got up from the grave, after purchasing our salvation, with all power in his hands. Just the joy of that victory gave Sunday a kind of gravitational pull on the people of God to meet to celebrate that marvelous victory.

The text also reports that this worship was not a morning worship but an evening worship.

Evening worship at that time was very important. They met in the evening because it was the only time that certain people in that family of faith could come. Usually it was the only time that the slaves would be free from their work to attend. They did not have the flexibility of schedule that perhaps others had because their day was controlled by their masters. But the church thought enough of these slaves that they were willing to alter their meeting time so that all of the family members could be present. Look at the church adjusting itself to meet the needs of all of its members, even the "least of of these."

Once they all arrived they would have what was called the Love Feast. This was not the Lord' Supper. This was something separate. The Lord's supper would usually follow the Love Feast. The Love Feast was a common meal shared by the community of faith celebrating their love for one another in Christ Jesus. This meal is much like the meals that some contemporary churches often have when they eat together as a congregation on special occasions. Sometimes the church is critiqued for meeting, greeting and eating. However, there is nothing wrong with the church meeting, greeting and eating. It only becomes a problem if that's all the church does. If you only meet, greet and eat and just decide the next time to meet, greet and eat then you don't understand the commission given by Christ.

But there is something really valuable about eating a meal together. Usually when you invite someone to eat a meal with you, you don't invite your enemies because it's bad for digestion. You usually invite people you want to eat with because eating a meal is a very intimate event. When you are eating you have tendency to relax, to let your hair down, to take your mask off, to run the risk of being yourself. And when you open up like that you provide the opportunity for a greater sense of intimacy. So when the people of God got together for the love feast, one of the reasons they did it was to enhance a sense of intimacy between one another.

Church is more than just showing up so that you and God can have fellowship with one another. It is also so that you can come and connect with other family members in the faith and take the risk of being yourself.

Some people's interpretation of Christianity can make a hypocrite out of you. They will make you think that because you are a Christian you are supposed to be perfect and, if you're not careful, you will make the mistake of trying to be perfect just so you can fool them. You are not perfect and nothing in your life is perfect but some people will make you think that it's supposed to be perfect. So you will pretend like all is well when it is not. You have to keep a mask on to keep up appearances and pretend like you've got it all together. In that kind of environment you are too afraid to be honest and real because as soon as you tell the truth about yourself and your situation people look down on you or go public with your issues. The church has to learn to be more transparent. We have to create an environment where believers don't have to be phony so that there can be a greater sense of intimacy among ourselves. The Love Feast was so that they could have a meal designed, in part, to create a greater sense of intimacy among the believers.

There was another practical reason for the Love Feast as well. The Love Feast was there for the "least of these." There were slaves among the congregation that the Love Feast took into consideration. The reason why the Love Feast was so important to the slave is because oftentimes, the Love Feast was the only substantial meal that many slaves ate all week long. It was the church's way of providing for those who were a part of the family. This is a reminder to those of us in the congregation who are being bountifully blessed by God that one of the reasons why God has blessed us with so much more than we need is not so that we can go around bragging about how much more we have but so that we can be a blessing to somebody else, especially those of our Christian family who are less fortunate than we are. Paul says that we are the body of Christ (1 Cor. 12:12). One thing that is true about a physical body is that if there is pain in one part of the body the entire body feels it. Once the body feels it, the body begins to marshal the necessary resources from throughout the body to help heal the hurt area. The body of Christ should be that way. When there is joy in the body the entire body of believers should share the joy. And where there is pain and need the body should be sensitive to that need and marshal the necessary resources needed to minister to that part of the body that needs help and healing.

When the feast was over, evening came and it was time for worship. No doubt believers came from miles around for this special worship service. Can't you see them, crowds of people climbing the stairs to the upper room on the third floor of a borrowed house? In the midst of the crowd came a young man, a slave named Eutychus. We don't know if he came by himself or with his family. However, one thing implied in the text is that he came for the same reason that everyone else had come. He came to hear the last words of a great man.

I can imagine Eutychus climbing the stairs with others and sitting down to the Love Feast eating with the others. Once the meal had ended, like the others, he was ready with tip toe anticipation to participate in the special worship experience. Imagination suggests that he finds a seat among the crowd crammed in there to hear the Apostle Paul. He sits on the edge of his seat because he is determined to hear every word that slips from the lips of the preacher because, after all, it is the famed Apostle Paul. He has heard about Paul and no doubt, has witnessed Paul in action in ministry. So here is a man he admired, one he looked up to, perhaps even wanted to be like one day. He was determined to hear every word.

The service was rather long that night for Paul had much to share. I am confident that under the circumstances no one complained. It was a special moment to hear a special man deliver a special message. Besides, in those days and in that culture, they did not share our preoccupation with time. Yet, even in a culture not preoccupied with time, it appears that time began to get the best of young Eutychus. He had good intentions. He had every intention of hearing every syllable uttered by the man of God. But too many things began to conspire against his desire to remain awake. The night was long. His body was tired. His stomach was full from the Love Feast. The place was packed. The room was stuffy and warm. The upper level was lit with candles whose flames shimmered with an almost hypnotic glow. He could feel the pull of sleep heavy on him. But he was determined to hear the words of Paul so he shook it off and slid up to the edge of his seat focusing to remain alert. But it was warm, he was tired and full, the place was crowded warm and the lights were dancing about and he was getting sleepy.

However, imagination suggests that because he was determined to remain awake he changed positions. He got up from the seat he was sitting in, in midst of the crowd and decided to move to a window. He sits precariously on the edge in the window. He did it so that the breeze blowing through would keep him awake because he wasn't going to miss the last words of this great man Paul.

But as Eutychus listened to Paul's lengthy address, despite his best efforts, it was not long before he found himself once again fighting the specter of sleep. His eyelids felt heavy as sandbags, his shoulders drooped and slumped with fatigue, his head bobbed and jerked forward and backward, this way and that as he struggled to remain awake. And soon he succumbed, closed his eyes, dropped his head in the locks of his shoulders and drifted off into a deep, intoxicating, satisfying sleep.

Suddenly there was a gasp followed by a loud scream as someone watched Eutychus lean out the window, lose his balance and tumble headlong to the street three stories below. And when he hit the ground Luke says that he was dead. And if anyone would know he was dead, it had to be Luke. After all, Luke was a physician.

The meeting stops abruptly and the mass of people rushed down where Eutychus laid. At first the people were certain that it was a lost cause. But Paul soon came and stretched out over the body of the boy and embraced him like Elijah and Elisha did to a dead boy in days of old (1 Kings 17:19-22, 2 Kings 4:32-35). Lying over the dead body of this slave boy soon Paul stepped back and declared, "Don't be afraid. He's alive!" After they lifted Eutychus up alive, Paul and the others returned upstairs where Paul continued fellowshipping with the people until the wee hours of the early morning. And Eutychus was taken home alive, to the sheer delight of the fellowship, his family and friends.

Now this is a simple story but it is not simply a story. It must be difficult to read this story without many of us seeing a bit of our own bio-data in it. No doubt all of us can identify with young Eutychus in this story. Who among us has never had to fight sleep during some worship service? And no doubt we struggled to stay awake because we have been taught, and rightly so, that regardless of how comfortable the church house gets-with padded pews, and air conditioned atmosphere- the church is no place to go to sleep.

Yes, Eutychus falls asleep in church. But lest we be too hard on Eutychus, we must acknowledge that he may have fallen asleep, but at least he was there. This puts to shame those believers who are awake but all too often absent. He may have fallen asleep, but while there, he was in a better position to hear the word of God than those who are absent.

Now, I am not trying to let Eutychus off the hook. The church is still no place to sleep. If there is ever a time you need to be awake, it is in church. And it is unfortunate when folks come to church and fall asleep. But before I talk about the ills of being asleep when you ought to be awake, we must be honest and admit that one of the reasons some people go to sleep in some churches, is not because they fall asleep, but because they are put to sleep.

Sometimes churches can be guilty of having a dead, drab, dusty, sedate, outdated, unchanged, predictable, irrelevant worship experience. They just put things on automatic pilot and let them run as they always do. Parishioners show up like pre-programmed robots and mindlessly go through the regiment of ritualistic worship. Quality is of no consequence, mediocrity is the status quo. That church is satisfied with just enough to get by.

Efforts are half-hearted, music is mediocre, preaching is irrelevant, praise is absent or inauthentic and the entire effort is infected by a ho-hum attitude. No wonder people get bored and fall asleep. Sometimes it is just because we lack relevance, excitement, variety, effort, preparation, innovation, authenticity and creativity. So preacher, why do you get upset when someone falls asleep if you have just slopped together a cliché ridden sermon (the night before) that reflects little thought or imagination? Choir, why are you surprised when people nod off as you sing, when your effort seems half hearted and you sing from your throat and never from your heart? Ushers, do you greet the worshippers with a smile or do you look like you wish you were somewhere else? Worshippers are you glad to be in the house of the Lord anticipating an encounter with the creator and savior or do you look indifferent, detached, lethargic, lackadaisical, and apathetic? Boredom is just as contagious as excitement. Yes, sometimes those who come do not fall asleep in church they are put to sleep by the church!

Churches can become so irrelevant at times that not only do they put worshippers to sleep, the put entire communities to sleep. The reason why sometimes the community is asleep as it relates to the church is because the church may not be having any meaningful impact in the community around it. And when the church makes no kingdom impact in the community around it, then when it comes to the things of God the community is put to sleep.

Still, I am not prepared to put all the blame on the church for sleeping parishioners. While the church must take some of the responsibility, you as an individual worshipper have to take some of the responsibility too. If you are going to maximize your worship experience, have a transformative encounter with the living Lord, leave after the benediction and have an impact in the world, then you are going to have to do some practical things.

The first practical thing you are going to have to do is prepare for worship. I learned a long time ago that any place worth going to is worth preparing for. Anything that matters to you, you usually take the time to prepare for. You prepare for school, work, travel, entertainment, attending cultural events. Anything worth participating in is worth preparing for.

When I was growing up I remember my parents being masterful at preparing for worship. I remember what it was like in our house the night before the Lord's Day worship. Saturday night was a night of preparation. Mama would be in the kitchen getting Sunday's food ready for the Sunday meal. Daddy would be reminding all six of us to make sure that we prepare for Sunday, that we take a bath and lay out our clothes and shine our shoes so that all things would be in order for the next morning. We would get in bed at a reasonable hour and sleep the night away. And when the first penciling light of day streaked across the horizon and Sunday morning came on a rope of twilight, daddy would come to our rooms and wake us up for morning prayer. You see, my daddy knew that while it was important that we get our clothes together for worship, it was also important to get our souls ready for worship. Not only did we get sleep to prepare our bodies, but we said our prayers to prepare our spirits. It might be easier to worship if we would spend time at the feet of God before we get to the house of God. Better still, if we actively walked with God during the week then it wouldn't be difficult to praise God on Sunday because it's difficult to walk with the Lord all week long and then come to church on Sunday and not have anything to thank God for. Too many people come to church and expect the worship leaders to set them on fire. But if we would walk with God every day of the week we would already be on fire and when we got to worship all the worship leaders would have to do is fan the flame! One secret to staying awake is to prepare for worship.

But if you are going to remain awake and benefit from transformational worship, not only must you prepare for worship but you must also participate in worship. Worship is not you coming to see what God is going to do. Worship is God coming to see what you are going to do. We need to understand that worship is not entertainment. It is not something you simply come and witness. When it comes to worship saints are not to spectate but to participate. Worship is something you do and no one can do it for you. Worship is both attitude and action. Worship is not something dead and cold, but passionate and participatory. Worship is not to be done with the mind alone, but with emotions and the whole body, also. Worship can be silent, still and planned. But it is also loud, spontaneous and physical. In a real sense, worship is like a bank account, if you want to get something out of it you have got to put something into it. When you unashamedly open yourself up to the presence and power of the living God, God can and will touch you, lift you, fill you and move you in ways you did not think were possible.

If the reason why the church decided to worship on Sunday was because it is the day that the Lord took the sting out of death, robbed the victory from the grave, took the keys of death and hell from the enemy's waist, snatched the crown from Satan's head, and declared all power was in his hand, then that means that when we come together for worship we have something to celebrate! Our savior lives and reigns supreme! And after six days of being tossed and driven by mean bosses and fretful circumstances, after six days of burden bearing and heavy load sharing, after six days of hell on the job or even hell at your house, Sunday morning serves to remind us that we serve a Lord that even death can't handle. And if he can conquer death, he can help you triumph over sin, sickness, sadness, sorrow and circumstances. That alone ought to make you want to participate and give God some praise! Yes, you can stay awake if you participate.

But I don't want to leave you with the impression that the only kind of sleep that this text can talk about is physical sleep. You see, sleep can mean just being unaware of what is going on around you. That means you can have your eyes wide open and still be fast asleep. But the church can't afford to be asleep. If there is ever a time that the church needs to be awake and aware, it is now. Listen, we can't afford to be asleep. We can't afford to walk around with our eyes closed. We can't afford to be apathetic, indifferent, unconcerned and uninformed. If there is one thing this story is recorded to remind us is, it is that it's dangerous to be asleep when you ought to be awake.

Consider what happened to Eutychus. First of all, the text points out that because he fell asleep, he missed God's message. Whenever you allow yourself to fall asleep when you ought to be awake, then you might miss an important lesson or word from the Lord. You see while he was asleep, Paul was preaching, which means that he missed a word from the Lord. And what Paul had to share was surely of the utmost importance. Remember, Paul was preaching there for the last time. And I am certain that he was trying his best to share with his listeners as much important information about living God's way as he could. That was why Paul preached so long. He tried to get as much to the people as he could before he was forced to depart the following day. We don't know what Paul said. But whatever it was, Eutychus missed part of it because he went to sleep.

Followers of Christ are the wrong people to be sleeping. The Father, the Kingdom and the world needs Christians who are wide awake, Christians who are alive, alert, aware, engaged, informed, and involved. In a world like ours, with a mission like ours sleeping churches just won't do. Heaven is too real, hell is too hot, time is too short, the devil is too busy, drugs are to prevalent, HIV is too deadly, poverty is too pervasive, prisons are too full, babies out of wedlock are too many, the poor are too exploited, the economy is too bad, racism is too real and Black folks are too far behind for the church to be sitting in the sanctuary sound asleep! Stay awake!

We need to be awake because we need to hear from heaven. When you go through life asleep you miss the voice of God and you miss out on the life lessons that the Master is trying to teach you.

We need to be awake because we need to remain aware of the needs of fellow human beings around us. Sleeping people live only for themselves and are insensitive to others around them.

We need to remain awake because if evil isn't sleeping we can't afford to sleep either. Too often darkness persists because while evil is awake and busy, good folks are fast asleep. Whatever you do, don't fall asleep!

Now, this would be just a humorous story about a boy who fell asleep in church if it weren't for one little detail in the text. The text says that Eutychus went to sleep and then he fell. Now perhaps we could laugh about the fact that he went to sleep if he had just gone to sleep but he went to sleep and then he fell. Whatever else that detail reveals, it ought to alert us to the truth that whenever you fall asleep when you ought to be awake you set yourself up for a fall. The Bible says that because Eutychus went to sleep he fell. And when he fell it was from the dangerous height of three stories which led to his death. Sleep will make you fall.

Students fall behind in their studies.

Achievers fall below their potential.

Young people fall into a life of crime.

Spouses fall away from one another.

Friends fall out with one another.

Christians fall into sin.

Young women fall for the tricky lines of smooth talking, sweet smelling, Barry White sounding men who don't have their best interests at heart.

Young men fall for the seductive lines of gold-digging women whose greatest concern is not the quality of their character but the frequency of their cash flow.

Churches fall into the trap of conforming to the status quo and end up becoming the world's echo instead of the Lord's voice.

Whenever you fall asleep when you should be awake you set yourself up for a fall!

Well, if you were to look deeper in the text you might see something else quite disturbing. As I was pondering this passage I could see in my mind's eye this young boy Eutychus perched precariously on the edge of that third story window. Then I saw him fall. When he fell, I wondered, what were all the adults doing while this child was sitting in such a dangerous place that led to his fall? Then it dawned on me that perhaps he fell because the adults who were present were so busy doing something else that no one was paying attention to the place and plight of this young boy.

How often have our children ended up in dangerous situations and then end up seriously hurting themselves because we adults are too busy doing other things? Too busy climbing corporate ladders. Too busy pursuing personal dreams. Too busy making money so we can buy more stuff. Too busy looking for a spouse because you are tired of being a single parent. Too busy going to school. Too busy going to church. Too busy doing a good thing that we forget about the best thing, and that's our children. If you are so busy doing good things that you can't watch your child then you need to reprioritize your life. It is possible to do good things and watch our children, too, so let's not get so busy that we forget to watch the window.

Notice also that the text says Eutychus fell from the window. He didn't jump from the window. He fell. He didn't mean to end up where he ended up, dead below a third story window.

Imagine for a moment why young Eutychus might have chosen to sit in that window so dangerously high above the ground. Perhaps he sat in the window because it was too crowded everywhere else. So he was just trying to deal with a crowded house. Or maybe he sat in the window because it was warm in the atmosphere and he chose a place that would keep him cool and awake. Whatever the reason he chose to sit in the window, it could very well be that he sat there because he was trying to deal with an environment that he didn't even create!

And the truth of the matter is that too often we blame our children for choosing "windows" to sit in, precarious places of danger that are bound to lead to hurt, hardship or harm without understanding why. Yes, sometimes it is because they are disobedient and hard headed. But could it be that many of them are just trying to cope with environments that they didn't create?

Look at that young boy on the corner slinging dope. It against the law, it's dangerous, it's not good, it's not right. It puts him precariously on the edge of the law, but every young dope dealer is not on the corner slinging dope because his goal is to poison his community. Some are out there, in their poverty stricken neighborhoods, with broken homes, absent fathers, violent gangs, crowded, substandard schools and indifferent leaders trying their best to cope with an environment that they didn't create.

Look at the young girl in the same type of neighborhood who's sleeping around every time you turn around, placing herself precariously on the edge of teen pregnancy, or some STD or even HIV/AIDS. She's not usually doing it because she's just some out of control, irresponsible nymphomaniac. She may be engaging in survival sex because she doesn't see any other way to survive. It doesn't make sense, it's not good, there is no future in it, but she's just trying to cope with an environment that she didn't create.

There is an almost endless list of children who have chosen to sit on the edge of a precarious situation, trying their best to deal with situations that they did not create. You'd be surprised where you'd choose to sit if the situation became desperate enough. Truth is, young and old, rich and poor, Black and White, saved and unsaved, have fallen out of windows because, for some reason or the other, they chose to sit on the edge. Eutychus sat on the edge and he fell.

But I love what Paul and the church did once they learned of his fall. They went to the door. They didn't just go to the window. I'm afraid that going to the window is too often what we do when folks fall. And when we go, we rarely go to assess the fall to see how we can help. Folks usually go to the window because it's safe. They can see the problem but they are far enough away not to have to get involved. They usually go to the window, say a prayer and go back to having church.

But others go to the window to gossip and criticize. Can't you hear them talking, "You ain't gonna believe this. Come over here and look out the window!"

"How did he get down there all broken and hurt?"

"I heard he was sitting in this window, right here on the edge. He had no business sitting here. I don't feel sorry for him."

"Huh, serves him right. You would never catch me sitting in no window like that."

You know how folks can be. But what I like about Paul and this church is that they didn't go to the window, they went to the door. The window gives you to chance to condemn and criticize those who've fallen. But the door gives you access to reach out and help those who have fallen. That's what Paul and the church he was preaching to did. They went out to where the fallen man was and got involved in trying to help him recover from his fall!

That's what the church is called to do. We are not called to condemn those who have fallen and been severely damaged by the fall. We are challenged to take the time and the risk to go where they are and do what we can to restore them to wholeness.

Paul and the others went to the window. Luke says the boy was dead. But no matter how hopeless the boy looked, the text says that when Paul got there he laid himself on the boy and threw his arms around him. We don't know how long Paul lay there. We don't know how long he put his arms around him. But when Paul got finished the boy who everyone thought was hopelessly gone got up alive!

That's what we have to do. We've got to refuse to give up on the fallen. We have to find them and come close enough to put our arms around them, close enough to speak words of encouragement to them, close enough to breathe life into them, and with the help of God, give them power to get up!

There are fallen people who need us to embrace them with words that empower. We need to say to that young girl with children out of wedlock, "We know that you are struggling. We know that to some you are just a statistic. We know that people have given up on you and you are ready to give up on yourself. But in the name of Jesus, we are here now, and if you let us we will hold on to you until you can stand!"

We've got to say to that high school dropout, "If you want to get up, we have GED programs to help you get your diploma. We have job training, to help you become employable, and scholarships to help you go to college. You can make it. We believe in you."

We have to say to the ex-offender, "we are not going to hold your past over your head. We will not only help prepare you for life outside, but we will fight for legislation that restores your voting rights and change your legal status so you won't have to keep being punished even after you are freed."

We've got to say to the crack addict, the homeless, the abused, the wayward and the lost, to those with full bank accounts but empty souls, "we are not perfect, but we have come in the name of Jesus to tell you that all is not lost. We will not stand in the window; we have come through the door to see about you." And most of all, we have to tell all who don't know the Lord, that if you really want to live, if you really want to rise, if you really want to get up, real life is found in a personal relationship with Jesus Christ!

The truth is that if you look closely at this text you can see redemptions' story in the story of this fallen boy. In fact, he represents the plight of all men and women throughout the ages. He fell three stories to the ground and those three stories can represent three dimensions of time—past, present and future. He fell from a window; we all fell from grace. He fell to his death; we were all dead in sin. Eutychus was dead but Paul ran down the stairs to see about him. All of humanity was dead in our sins, but Jesus came all the way down from heaven down to see about us. Paul stretches himself out over Eutychus and gave him new life. Jesus was stretched out on Calvary that we might have eternal life!   The good news is that for all who have fallen into sin and are dead in sins there is a Savior, Christ the Lord, who if you repent of your sins and trust in him, he will give you a brand new life, Gods' kind of life, eternal life!

Honoring 'The Call'

Romans 10:15

15And how shall they preach, except they be sent? as it is written, How beautiful are the feet of them that preach the gospel of peace, and bring glad tidings of good things!

Is it just me or does it seem like everyone wants to be a preacher these days? I remember when I was contemplating my call to preach. Just about every preacher I spoke to had one thing in common—initially, none of them wanted to preach. They all ran from the call; some ran for years. I could identify because I was not interested in preaching either.

I had made up my mind that I would be a lawyer. My father had been a preacher and pastor and I had seen how some church folks had treated him. So, I was determined that I would never be a preacher. I would be a lawyer. That way, I could work when I wanted, make as much money as I wanted, drive what I wanted, dress the way I wanted, live the way I wanted and if I did not want to deal with people, I did not have to. And the good thing was I could still do something that would be of some benefit to the community. But I was not, under any circumstances, going to be a preacher. I didn't care how many old saints in my church said I had "the mark," whatever that was. However, once the Lord got a hold of my heart and life, I didn't feel like I had a choice. I didn't choose it; it chose me. I didn't take up preaching; it took me up. Even if I resisted the call and became a rich, successful attorney, I knew I would be miserable. I started feeling that call when I was about 18. I finally yielded when I was about 20. That was just over 30 years ago.

I started preaching because I had to! It was not for fame or fortune. My soul was going to have no peace until I yielded to the Lord's will. I would go where God wanted, do what God wanted, and live the way God chose. I was compelled to preach, and I come from a tradition where people preach because they are called by God to preach.

As I have already stated, back then, nobody I knew really wanted to preach. But these days it seems as if everyone wants to preach. It appears that every time I turn around someone from my congregation is telling me that they believe they are called to preach. Now, some folks say that is just the sign of a healthy church. Others have suggested that so many are answering the call because God is doing a new thing. The world is so messed up that if there is ever a time we need preachers to preach God's truth it's now! All of that may be true. If it is, praise the Lord! Whatever God is behind, I am for it.

But I have a suspicion that there is another reason why some are claiming they have been called to preach. They are claiming a call because they are attracted to what seems to surround preaching and preachers these days. Television, videos, magazines, DVD's, and YouTube have made many preachers stars. These days, being a preacher is associated with being popular and rich! I suspect that many people, whether consciously or unconsciously, are drawn to this image of the preacher. Mega churches, expensive cars, fashionable clothes, high profile interviews, personal websites, TBN appearances, radio broadcasts, vast clerical fanbases, visions of hobnobbing with the rich and famous, first-class flying or private jets, crowd adoration and a host of other things associated with fame and fortune have drawn people to the preaching ministry with an almost irresistible gravitational pull.

Now, if the Lord blesses your ministry with any or all of the previously mentioned things, may the Lord keep on blessing you. I hope you use it all to God's glory. However, it is one thing to come to the ministry and have your fruitfulness (work) bring attention to you; it's another thing to come to the ministry seeking fame, fortune and notoriety. Such persons do not sense a divine call to the ministry and are not stirred to ask, "What's in me for it?" But they are lured to the ministry by the prospect of the glitter and glamour of ministry and are moved to ask, "What's in it for me?"

There are pastors who have the difficult responsibility of helping men and women discern their call. It is incumbent upon us to take the task very seriously and not get caught up in personal ego gratification that so many are being called under our ministries. We must do a thorough job of helping our parishioners understand whether they are hearing from the Lord, enamored by what they believe are the trappings of ministry or wrestling with some issue or event that they have spiritualized into a call.

In the final analysis, only God knows for certain who is sent by God and who just went for themselves. But we who pastor have the responsibility to do our best to help those who come to us regarding the preaching ministry to understand the nature of "the call" and the nature of "their call."

Here are some suggestions that can assist us:

1. Create a system that helps parishioners discern the authenticity and nature of their call. Some denominations already have them within their ecclesiastical structure. But I am part of a denomination that does not have a reliable, uniform approach to helping people understand the call to preach. In my denomination, one could literally be saved one week, say they are called to preach the next week, preach their initial sermon the following week, and pastor a church shortly thereafter!

2. Create a system that insists that certain meaningful requirements be met before persons do their initial sermon and are licensed. Sometimes the very fact that a person knows that they have to complete certain requirements and uphold certain standards before they are allowed to preach or get licensed helps weed out those who are motivated by the wrong things. If nothing else, it at least weeds

out the lazy ones who are called! Your system should include a strong emphasis on the importance of theological education. A call to preach is a call to prepare. And we ought to let those who cannot complete a three-year seminary program know that they can still learn and grow and they must!

Also, if they have not, require that persons faithfully participate in some ministry of the church that you select. Check their level and quality of participation. Are they faithful? Do they get along with others? Are they professional in their dealings with church members and officers?

3. Provide or guide them to opportunities for them to preach in settings other than the pulpit.

If a person who claims to be called to preach is unwilling to preach in preaching labs, at nursing homes, Salvation Army facilities, street corners, prisons, jails, etc., they need clarification on what the call to preach concerns. If they only want to preach at "prime time" then they may be preaching for the wrong reason. A preacher will preach anywhere.

4. Help them understand that most preachers do not have mega churches, large salaries, and name recognition. The average church has fewer than 250 members. If they just want to be famous and rich, suggest that they choose something other than preaching. Also, make clear that every preacher called is not called to pastor!

5. Model before your congregation the priorities of a preacher called to preach. A pastor/preacher whose conversation is primarily about money, clothes, cars, getting the best preaching engagements, and how many members are in their congregation but rarely about family life, service, sacrifice, faithfulness, prayer, personal holiness, saving souls, righting wrongs, and personal balance is a poor role model for parishioners contemplating and/or trying to be faithful to their call to preach. Persons called to ministry need the assistance of

pastors and others who can help them discern how to faithfully live out their calling. If you are one of the persons who is to provide such assistance, make sure that you have a written, systematic, and well thought out plan to help those whom the Lord has placed in your care. The plan should be malleable enough to assist persons of all ages.

A Remedy for a Snake Bite

Acts 28:1-6

1 Once safely on shore, we found out that the island was called Malta. 2 The islanders showed us unusual kindness. They built a fire and welcomed us all because it was raining and cold. 3 Paul gathered a pile of brushwood and, as he put it on the fire, a viper, driven out by the heat, fastened itself on his hand. 4 When the islanders saw the snake hanging from his hand, they said to each other, "This man must be a murderer; for though he escaped from the sea, the goddess Justice has not allowed him to live." 5 But Paul shook the snake off into the fire and suffered no ill effects. 6 The people expected him to swell up or suddenly fall dead; but after waiting a long time and seeing nothing unusual happen to him, they changed their minds and said he was a god.

The main character in our text is the famed Apostle Paul. Paul was once a zealous persecutor of the church but as a consequence of a cataclysmic conversion experience on the Damascus Road, (Acts 9) Paul is no longer a persecutor of the gospel he is a perpetuator of the gospel. And with the same burning zeal and passionate desire that he once attacked the church, he has now dedicated his life to establishing the church and spreading the good news throughout the known world.

At the time of this text Paul is nearing the end of his series of missionary journeys. Paul has always had a desire to go to Rome and preach and then to Spain. Now Paul is on his way to Rome. His dream is finally coming true, but with a twist. You see, Paul never dreamed he would be going to Rome in the state that he is in, for Paul is on his way to Rome as a prisoner. But you know, God moves in mysterious ways. God has a way of getting you where he wants you to go but he doesn't always get you there the way you expect. Still, while Paul may be a prisoner on his way to Rome, there is at least one advantage to going to Rome as a prisoner. If Paul had gone as a free man, he would have had to pay his own way but since he is traveling as Rome's prisoner, the Roman government is footing the bill!

Paul not only never dreamed of going to Rome as a prisoner but I suspect that he never anticipated the great trials he would have to experience on the way to Rome. Paul has been sailing to Rome in a ship. And at the time of our text Paul and others are at the tail end of a horrendous storm and tremendous ship wreck. This incident was not some minor storm that simply blew them off course to another destination. But this storm almost took their lives. The storm literally shredded their ship to pieces, and they only survived by some jumping into the water and swimming to shore while those who could not swim made it to shore on broken pieces of the ship.

Now in our text they are cold, wet, bone weary, muscle tired, and anxious because they have landed on an unknown island. The storm has been catastrophic and has disoriented them so that they have no idea where they are. They are literally at the mercy of strangers. And once those strangers show up, Paul and the others soon learn that they are on an Island called Malta.

The natives of the land are referred to in the King James Version of the Bible as barbarians. The term barbarian has come to mean people who are unsavory, uncouth and uncivilized. But the natives of Malta are anything but uncivilized. When they come out to meet these shivering, shipwrecked, seafarers, they do not come to threaten their lives, take their goods or take advantage of their vulnerable state. Instead Paul says they show them unusual kindness, care and compassion. These total strangers could have treated them with violence, contempt or even indifference. But instead, they reached out in love and concern.

That is what our world needs more of. We have become so suspicious these days, suspicious and selfish. We don't want to reach out to anyone we don't know or who at least doesn't look like us. What we need more of is the compassion characterized by these natives in our text. I know it's dangerous and folks can be cunning, but compassion requires risk. And every now and then, we need to take the risk of reaching out, in the name of Jesus.

The sad thing is that these strangers treated Paul better than his own people did. If you read the record, once Paul became a Christian, Paul was often persecuted by fellow Jews, the chosen ones, the people of God, the ones who had access to the creator, the ones who should have been showing the nations how to behave. And yet, Paul was treated better by these pagans.

We believers can learn a lesson from that. Sometimes folks that are not believers can put believers to shame. Sometimes folks that are not Christians can out-Christian Christians when it comes to at least behaving like a Christian. Consider that unbeliever standing in a long line at the grocery store being patient, considerate and kind, and you, a believer, huffing and puffing, shifting from foot to foot, cussing under your breath, impatiently standing in line and when you get to the cashier you got an attitude that Jesus ain't got nothing to do with. Or consider how that homeless man will scoot over and give space on a park bench so he and another homeless man can get some sleep but sometimes we church folk got a problem moving over on a church bench so another believer can sit next to us in worship. Or consider the countless folks who don't know Christ but are standing up for folks that can't stand up for themselves, giving, caring and sharing with those in need, while too many believers are too busy looking out for number one. Sometimes the unbeliever can out-Christian the Christian and put us to shame.

Well, the natives were kind and showed their kindness in tangible ways. The text says that it was cold and raining so they took the nearly 300 strangers and put them under a shelter and then they built a bonfire to make them dry and keep them warm. It was no small matter to reach out to almost 300 unknown, unexpected strangers.

Once they got fairly settled and situated it looked like all was well, at least for a while. But no sooner had Paul gotten himself together than a snake enters the picture. You know, it seems like since the beginning of time, snakes have had a way of showing up and messing things up. Paul had just finished dealing with a storm and here comes a snake. Ain't that just like life? As soon as you get on the other side of one bit of trouble here comes something else. You can hardly catch your breath or get your feet up under you before another test or trial comes. Sometimes they even come in rapid succession, riding piggy back on one another like waves on the sea shore. If it ain't one thing, it's another.

Paul had just escaped a storm and now he is bitten by a snake. Now I thought I would bring this snake bite scenario up because I want you to realize something. Everybody wants a wonderful and blessed life. And I pray that your life is wonderfully blessed. But life doesn't come without snake bites. I hate to bring you bad news, but you can't get through life without some snake bites. I don't care who you are, you are going to have to deal with snake-like situations, poisonous predicaments and even poisonous people. All snakes don't crawl on their bellies; some snakes are of the two legged variety!

There are going to be times in your life when snakes are going to try to inject poison into you, your attitude, your family, your finances, your efforts, your relationships, your goals, your hopes and your dreams. We all stand to get bitten somewhere along the line. But I think that Paul teaches us some valuable lessons about snakes and snake bites. I think Paul can teach us a remedy for a snake bite.

Notice how it happened. The text says that Paul was carrying sticks to the fire designed to warm him and others. Now, I like what I see Paul doing. Paul is bringing sticks to the fire, a fire that is designed to enhance the quality of life for others. He is just one man, but he is doing his part to add to the fire. He is the type of person that isn't content with feeling the warmth of the fire without making a contribution to the flame.

Paul is a good example of the way people ought to be. But the fact is, there are too many folks who like to warm themselves by the fire but are not willing to bring any sticks to the flame. They like titles but they won't do the task. They want recognition but not responsibility. They want to benefit without making any contributions, like crowns but no crosses, desire glory but no gall, want gain without pain. But if you want to warm yourself by the fire the least you ought to do is bring some sticks!

So many Christians want warm, anointed, exciting and relevant worship, but they won't pray, praise, or say "amen". They want to be associated with a church that is known for being about something, but they won't make a contribution to what it's about. They want a great church without being a great member. They won't give financially to its ministries but as soon as they get in trouble they want a contribution from its benevolence fund. Too many saints want something for nothing. They want power but they won't pray. They want to know the Word but they won't study the Word. They want a blessed life without living a holy life. They want a great marriage but they won't be a great spouse. They want children but they don't want to raise them. They want to be forgiven but they won't forgive. They want a job but they don't want to look for it. They want money but they don't want to work for it. They want a promotion on the job but they habitually come late and leave early. They want the grade but they don't want to study. We want the best but we want it for less. We want quality goods but at discount prices. In the words of Fredrick Douglass, "They want rain without thunder and lightning, crops without tilling up the soil, they want the beauty of the ocean without the roar of its many waters." Too many want something but we want it for nothing. But if you are going to benefit from the fire, the least you ought to do is put some sticks in the flames!

Paul could have come up with reasons for not contributing. He could have used his accomplishments and achievements to exempt him from carrying sticks. He was called as an Apostle of God. God had used him to heal the sick and raise the dead. He beckoned crowds to gather around and hear him speak and had with his words held them captive as if with a wizard's spell. He had planted churches, saved souls, turned cities upside down. But Paul remained humble because he knew that the power was not in him; the power was in the one who called him. Here we ought to be reminded that we should never become so important that there are some things that even God can't ask us to. We should never become so educated, acclimated, assimilated and important that we can't humbly serve. If you ever become too important to serve then that makes you better than Jesus. The scriptures declare this about the humility of Jesus: "Who, being in very nature God, did not consider equality with God something to be grasped, but made himself nothing, taking the very nature of a servant, being made in human likeness. And being found in appearance as a man, he humbled himself and became obedient to death– even death on a cross!" (Philippians 2:6-8 NIV) Servanthood was at the heart of the ministry of the master. We should never become so important that we can't carry some sticks to the flame.

Paul could have used his state as a prisoner to excuse him from bringing any sticks. He had chains and could have used the limitation of the chains as a reason for non-participation. There are many people who because of limitations conclude that since they can only do a little then they might as well not do anything. But don't let any limitations stop you from making a contribution. The fire needs small twigs as well as large limbs. Besides, what looks like little in the eyes of men, may be great in the eyes of God.

Paul got bitten while trying to carry sticks to the flame. In fact, in a real sense, that snake did not simply bite Paul while he was doing good. That snake bit Paul because he was doing good. Paul's hands are the type of hands that the snake hates. His hands are the kind that the enemy bites. The enemy doesn't bother hands that aren't about anything. He doesn't bite hands that are idle, apathetic, listless, lazy and limp with inactivity. He doesn't bite those hands because they are already poisoned!

The snake bites busy hands. It bites hands that are trying to do something to bless others and build the kingdom. Snakes get stirred up anytime your hands are busy doing something noble, godly, unselfish and worthwhile, something that edifies others and glorifies God. If you are committed to doing something that God will be pleased with expect to get bitten by snakes!

Paul put those sticks in the flame and before he could jerk his hand back, the text says that the snake bit him and was hanging there on this hand. It was bad enough that the snake bit him and tried to poison him, but consider the poisonous conclusions of those who were watching.

When they saw him get bitten they said "He must be a murderer. He escaped the sea, but justice has caught up with him to take him out." It's amazing the kind of conclusions folks will jump to. We have a sad habit of jumping to conclusions about what is going on in other folk's lives. We are so quick to think the worst of people rather than the best of people. We are just like the disciples who when they saw the man born blind said "Who sinned that this man is blind? Was it him? His parents?" Jesus said, in substance to them, "There you go jumping to conclusions again. There you go thinking the worst about someone and their situation again. This is not time to condemn him. This is a time to show compassion for him."

You know, if we were more inclined to show compassion for people, then when people experience misfortune we would be more inclined to pity the sufferer and stop praising the snake.

Paul was bitten. We are all going to be bitten. If you are serving God there is no way around it. So, how do you handle snake bite?

Well, the Bible says Paul simply shook it off. That is how we have got to learn to deal with snake bites. We have to bring a "shake it off" mentality to the attack of the enemy. When Paul got bitten he shook it off and kept on doing what he was doing. Now other folks around him, the text says, were standing around waiting for him to swell up and die. There is always someone who is watching, waiting and expecting the snake bite to take you out. They will always treat the attack of the enemy on your life as something fatal. There will always be people around who will predict and prognosticate about how your life is going to turn out. There are always people who, when they see you experience mishaps and misfortune, will predict that your life will turn out for the worst. But while they expected the worst, Paul didn't. Paul operated in faith and shook it off.

In fact, there is no indication in the text that Paul becomes anxious, upset, fearful or frustrated about the snake bite. He doesn't get angry and start blaming folks, God or the fire. He shook that snake off and kept on going. How could Paul shake it off? Where do you get the power to shake it off?

First, Paul could shake it off because Paul knew he had no control over the outcome. He kept on going because he had no control over how things would turn out. So, he decided to leave the outcome up to the Lord. In other words, Paul put his predicament in the Lord's hands. He couldn't handle it so he let God handle it. When you are bitten by the snake of negative circumstances, do your best and leave the outcome to God. Stop getting stressed out and bent all out of shape about things you have no control over. If you know God loves you, if you know God has got your back, if you know that there is nothing impossible for him, if you know all things work together for your good, if you know that he will not put on you any more than you can bear, and if you know that you are only responsible for the possible while God is responsible for the impossible, then you need to do what you can (shake it off, turn it loose, let it go) and leave the results to God! There is freedom in turning the things you have no control over into the hands of your loving, capable, caring, heavenly father, especially when you know he loves you and he has got you and your future in the palm of his hand. Shake it off!

The second thing that gave Paul the power to shake it off was that Paul knew disobedience didn't cause the bite. What I am suggesting is that perhaps Paul knew that he had not done anything wrong to bring about the snake bite situation. He had a clear conscience. When you know you are in the will of God, then you can shake off snake bites. The most blessed place to be is in the will of God. In fact, it is a blessing if you get bitten because you are doing God's will. The Bible says "Blessed are you when men shall revile you and persecute and say all manner of evil against you falsely for my sake... (Matthew 5:11)" It's easier to fight when you have a clear conscience.

But what if you are bitten because of disobedience? Let me tell you how to shake that off. The Bible declares, "If you confess your sins, he is faithful and just to forgive you and to cleanse you from all unrighteousness. (1 John 1:9)" You can still shake it off because of the blood! You may have to deal with the consequences but you don't have to live with the guilt. You can shake it off!

I believe that the third thing that gave Paul the power to shake it off is a promise he had. God had promised Paul that he was going to preach in Rome. Paul knew that God hadn't brought him that far to leave him. He knew that God hadn't brought him through the storm just to lose him to a snake. You can shake it off when you learn how to rest in the promises of God. If you know that God has given you an assignment, then when the enemy bites, shake it off and stick to your assignment, knowing that God hasn't brought you this far to leave you. If you are doing God's work, and are abiding in God's will, no matter what happens, you need to know that in the final analysis, God's will, will be done!

Shake it off! Whether you're lied on, talked about, conspired against, mistreated, misunderstood, left out, looedk over, forgotten, deserted, dogged out, excluded or kicked to the curb, just keep on doing the will of God and when the enemy bites you, shake it off and keep on going! Even Jesus got bitten on a Friday. Death bit him and Friday evening he hung his head and died. But early

Sunday morning he shook off death, stepped out of the grave, and declared that all power in heaven and earth is in his hand. He's alive and he's alive forever more! And if the Lord can shake off death, surely he can help you and me shake off the trials and tests of negative circumstances and the attacks of the enemy. So, shake it off, trust God, keep on doing God's will and leave the outcome to God.

Harder yet may be the fight
Right may often yield to might
Wickedness a while may reign
Satan's cause may seem to gain
But there is a God who rules above
With hand of power and heart of love
And if I'm right he'll fight my battle
I shall have peace some day[1]

---

1 Beams of Heaven as I Go Text: Charles Albert Tindley, ca 1906

THANK YOU, LORD!

Psalm 116

1I love the LORD, because he hath heard my voice and my supplications. 2Because he hath inclined his ear unto me, therefore will I call upon him as long as I live. 3The sorrows of death compassed me, and the pains of hell gat hold upon me: I found trouble and sorrow. 4Then called I upon the name of the LORD; O LORD, I beseech thee, deliver my soul. 5Gracious is the LORD, and righteous; yea, our God is merciful. 6The LORD preserveth the simple: I was brought low, and he helped me. 7Return unto thy rest, O my soul; for the LORD hath dealt bountifully with thee. 8For thou hast delivered my soul from death, mine eyes from tears, and my feet from falling. 9I will walk before the LORD in the land of the living. 10I believed, therefore have I spoken: I was greatly afflicted: 11I said in my haste, All men are liars. 12What shall I render unto the LORD for all his benefits toward me? 13I will take the cup of salvation, and call upon the name of the LORD. 14I will pay my vows unto the LORD now in the presence of all his people. 15Precious in the sight of the LORD is the death of his saints. 16O LORD, truly I am thy servant; I am thy servant, and the son of thine handmaid: thou hast loosed my bonds.

17I will offer to thee the sacrifice of thanksgiving, and will call upon the name of the LORD. 18I will pay my vows unto the LORD now in the presence of all his people. 19In the courts of the LORD's house, in the midst of thee, O Jerusalem. Praise ye the LORD.

I was raised in the Deep South and one of the characteristics of southern culture is good manners. I am not suggesting that no one has manners anywhere else but in the south, good manners are a must. One habit that was drilled in me as I was growing up is the habit of saying "Thank you." Whether I was talking to a sibling or total strangers, my parents impressed upon me that whenever anyone does anything nice for you, you ought to say thank you.

I am convinced that my parents tried to develop this habit in me not simply because they wanted me to be in the habit of saying thank you, but also because they wanted me to be thankful. They were not only after my having thankful habits but also my having a thankful spirit.

I believe that God desires the same of us. He wants us to learn to be thankful. When you lack an attitude of gratitude then you either become a chronic complainer, never satisfied, always grumbling and complaining, or you take blessings for granted; you don't complain about what you don't have, but you don't express gratitude for what you do have. God does not want us to be guilty of either of these attitudes. God wants us to have an attitude of gratitude. He wants us to learn how to be grateful.

One thing that has great potential to inspire gratitude in us, believe it or not, is trouble. In our text we have a psalm of thanksgiving that was inspired by someone who passes through a crisis of acute trouble and comes out of the other end of it full of thanksgiving. As we peruse the content of this psalm we will see that this man not only sings thank you but is also thankful!

As we begin reading the psalm you notice first, gratitude verbalized. Notice that the psalm begins with a great declaration of gratitude in verse 1 "I love the Lord…" Now I know at first glance that does not seem like a declaration of gratitude but rather a declaration of love. But when you look closer you discover that it is love cloaked in the garments of gratitude. The love declared here is a love "because of."

Our love for God is always essentially a love because of. In fact, the Bible makes it clear that the reason why we even love God in the first place is because he first loved us. And why did God first love us? It certainly wasn't because of anything that we have done. God loves us because it is God's nature to love. John writes that "God is love" (1John 4:8). So in a real sense, God just does what God is. God loves because it's God's nature to love. God loves us absolutely, totally, completely, unconditionally. There is nothing we can do to make him love us any more than he already does. And there is nothing we can do to love him any less! When you consider the fact that God has that kind of love for us, it just makes sense to love God in return.

The psalmist's song begins with a declaration of love cloaked in the garments of gratitude. "I love the Lord...." And what is the reason for his gratitude? Deliverance! His love is expressed in this psalm because God has delivered him. In verses 1 and 2 he sings, "I love the lord, for he heard my voice; he heard my cry for mercy. Because he turned his ear to me, I will call on him as long as I live." When this psalmist declares that God heard him when he cried out for mercy, he is not simply expressing that when he cried out, the audible vibrations caused by his voice were picked up by the ears of God. He is singing because God heard him and delivered him from trouble. Notice the nature of the deliverance he expresses in verse 8 "For you, O Lord, have delivered my soul from death, my eyes from tears, my feet from stumbling..." Here are the clues as to the nature of his deliverance. First, God delivered his soul from death. He means that God delivered him from a close call. Something threatened his life so directly that it almost killed him. He came so close to crossing over to the other side, that in the words of that great preacher Gardner Taylor, "he could feel the midst of the Jordan on his face." But just in the nick of time, God stepped in and delivered him from certain death.

I wonder if you can testify of how God has delivered you from a close call. Can you remember any close calls you have had in life, any near misses? Can you remember any situations where you know you should be dead, and you may have even thought you were as good as dead, but you cried out for mercy and the Lord stepped in right on time! Perhaps it was a sickness that was certain to take you out but miraculously our matchless healer delivered you. Perhaps you were in a car accident and you looked at the car with twisted metal and shattered glass, but then you looked at your body and there wasn't a scratch on it, and you knew the Lord had delivered you. Or maybe your marriage was as good as dead, but you cried out to the Lord and today your marriage is as solid as a rock. Perhaps you almost lost your business, your family, your chance at an education, you were falsely accused and almost lost your freedom, or you suffered a crisis that almost killed your hopes and dreams, but you cried out to the Lord and just in time he stepped and rescued you! If God has done anything like that for you then surely you ought to cry out in gratitude with the psalmist, "I love the Lord…"

God had delivered his eyes from tears. Something in his life, some sorrow or grief, caused him pain which led to tears. But he says that the Lord delivered his eyes from tears. That must mean that God healed the pain caused by the sorrow that led to the tears. God did not necessarily change the circumstances, but he did heal the wounds caused by the pain which led to the tears.

What a marvelous deliverance. Has God ever done that for you? Surely there are sorrows in our lives that have caused us great pain and have led to bitter tears. But like the psalmist we cried out to the Lord in the midst of our pain and the Lord delivered us! He may have delivered us by changing our circumstances. Once he changed our circumstances that thing or those people who caused us pain were removed from the midst and he healed us, hence drying our tears. But sometimes God doesn't change our circumstances. He heals us despite our circumstances and sets us free from tears. Someone walked out on you. It broke your heart into a million pieces. But you cried out to the Lord, and by his amazing grace he healed your broken heart. That person who left has never returned. But you aren't crying anymore. Or perhaps a dear loved one has died, someone you thought you just couldn't live without. The pain was so acute that you thought it would never go away. But you cried out to the Lord that he would have mercy on you. It took a while, but God has healed your heart and dried your tears. Your loved one was not returned to you, but God has delivered you. You ought to cry out "thank you!"

Third, the psalmist writes that he delivered his "feet from falling." The Lord kept him on his feet. The psalmist is expressing how he almost fell, but he didn't. He almost sinned, but he didn't. He almost gave up, but he didn't. He almost lost heart, but he didn't. And he is clear as to why he was able to keep his footing during a difficult time; it was nobody but the Lord who kept him on his feet.

Have you ever been there? Have you ever been in the midst of a trying trial, stressful struggle or tempestuous temptation and it caused you to stumble, threatening to make you utterly fall, but while you were stumbling you called on the Lord and he delivered your feet from falling? So many of us can testify that we made it through some hellish situations, not because we were so holy, or even because we were so strong, but because even though we started to stumble, when we cried out for help, the Lord mercifully kept us on our feet. Has he done it for you? It's good to thank God that you almost...but because of him, you didn't. Just think about where you would be right now if the Lord hadn't stepped in and kept you on your feet. Just think about the tangled mess of horrible circumstances you would be imprisoned in if the Lord had not stepped in and kept you from falling. You were lonely and stumbling and almost had an affair but you didn't. You were financially stumbling and almost stole money from your job but you didn't. You were stumbling emotionally, staggering from fear and feeling vulnerable and you almost went back to drinking and drugging, but you didn't. You experienced a life altering crisis and were stumbling so bad spiritually that you almost lost your faith, but you didn't. You almost...but you cried out to the Lord and somehow, some way,

God, by his mercy and grace, stepped in and kept you steady, stable and sane! You almost...but you didn't!

When God delivers you like that, when he gives you an almost testimony, then it's time to shout, "Thank you!" You can never really be the same after deliverance like that. In fact, the experience had such a profound effect on the psalmist that he further expresses his gratitude by declaring, "I will call on him as long as I live" (v. 2b).

But the psalmist not only verbalized his gratitude. If you keep reading the psalm you will not only see gratitude verbalized but you will also see evidence of gratitude concretized. When gratitude really gets a hold on you, then you don't just say, "thank you" but you do "thank you." In verse 12 the psalmist asks, "What shall I render unto the LORD for all his benefits toward me? Certainly, the psalmist does not really think that he can actually repay God. He is well aware that there is nothing he can do to pay off the debt and balance his account. God has been too good and he owes God too much. If he had a million lifetimes, he could never pay God back. That's not his intent. Still, his heart is so overwhelmed with gratitude that he is compelled to show it by doing something. The kind of love and goodness God has shown him deserves and indeed inspires some act of gratitude from his grateful heart.

So in verse 13 he sings, "I will lift up the cup of salvation and call on the name of the Lord." Here "the cup of salvation" seems to be a reference to the drink offering of wine poured out into a bowl by the altar when an animal sacrifice is given. So the grateful psalmist intends to give a gift to the Lord, a sacrifice. Not to pay him back, but to show his gratitude. He wanted to do something concrete as an expression of his gratitude. It was a sacrifice because as David declares in 2 Samuel 24:24, he would not give God anything that cost him nothing.

Surely we who are the great recipients of the goodness of God in Christ have a reason to give something to the Lord's service. It is one thing for us to come to worship with praise on our lips and joy in our dance as an expression of our gratitude. But shouldn't we have a gift in our hand, an offering given to the Lord inspired by our gratitude for His goodness and his grace?

A very interesting thing is declared by the psalmist in verses 14 and 18, "I will fulfill my vows to the Lord in the presence of his people." It seems clear that the psalmist is speaking of offering a concrete gift to the Lord in the presence of his people or in the public worship experience. He is so full of gratitude that he is glad to publicly show, with a concrete offering, his love and gratitude to a God who has been so good. But I also wonder if that phrase "I will keep my vows to the Lord," may be a reference to something he did that we often do when we are caught in the grip of trouble like the trouble God had delivered this psalmist from.

Could this be the psalmist remembering that when he was in the clutches of trouble, he cried out to the Lord saying in substance, "Lord, if you get me out of this, I promise you that I will..."? Have you ever made a vow like that? Have you ever, while in the teeth of the wind, promised the Lord something if he would deliver you? I suppose most all of us have. Sometimes it takes some trouble to bring us to our senses and remind us of how we ought to be living. Perhaps it takes a strong wind to blow some of us back on course. But let's be honest. The sad tragedy is that too often we make the promise while we are in the trouble, but as soon as we are delivered, we conveniently contract a serious case of amnesia and forget all about the promise we made. If this psalmist made that type of vow at least gratitude moved him to keep his!

Still, it appears that the greatest concrete expression of the psalmist's gratitude was not merely a material (or monetary) gift, but his greatest gift to God was himself! In verse 16a he declares "I am your servant..." The psalmist was at death's door, but he cried out to the Lord and the Lord delivered him. So grateful and thankful was this man that he was compelled to respond to such grace by offering himself to the Lord, "Lord I am your servant..." In light of the goodness of God, he reaffirms his commitment to God by recommitting himself afresh. Gratitude made him do it.

What about us? God has truly been good to us. Those who know and trust in Christ and in the cross of Calvary are especially aware of how good God has been to us. It was on Calvary that our Lord purchased our freedom with his precious blood and delivered us from eternal separation for our wonderful God. We can never pay him back. But he doesn't want us to. He wants us to receive his free gift of salvation and new life through him. He wants us to respond to his love and service with a life of love and service. He died for us so that we could live for him. And when I think of the great price he paid for me and how he delivered and keeps on delivering me by his mercy and grace, I am filled with gratitude and I say, "thank you" with my lips and with my life. I don't serve him because I'm trying to pay him back. I can't. I'm just grateful, and my service is just a huge "thank you" for all he has done for me. The song writer was right when he declared, "His love so unique, so divine, demands my life, my soul, my all." Thank you, Lord!

THE GREATEST GIFT OF ALL

Luke 2:8-20

8And there were in the same country shepherds abiding in the field, keeping watch over their flock by night. 9And, lo, the angel of the Lord came upon them, and the glory of the Lord shone round about them: and they were sore afraid. 10And the angel said unto them, Fear not: for, behold, I bring you good tidings of great joy, which shall be to all people. 11For unto you is born this day in the city of David a Saviour, which is Christ the Lord. 12And this shall be a sign unto you; Ye shall find the babe wrapped in swaddling clothes, lying in a manger. 13And suddenly there was with the angel a multitude of the heavenly host praising God, and saying, 14Glory to God in the highest, and on earth peace, good will toward men. 15And it came to pass, as the angels were gone away from them into heaven, the shepherds said one to another, Let us now go even unto Bethlehem, and see this thing which is come to pass, which the Lord hath made known unto us. 16And they came with haste, and found Mary, and Joseph, and the babe lying in a manger. 17And when they had seen it, they made known abroad the saying which was told them concerning this child. 18And all they that heard it wondered at those things which were told them by the shepherds. 19But Mary kept all these things, and pondered them in her heart. 20And the shepherds returned, glorifying and praising God for all the things that they had heard and seen, as it was told unto them.

I love the Christmas season. It's one of my favorite times of the year. I actually love to see the snow and experience the warmth that comes with special fellowship with family and friends. Unfortunately it is still true that the central message of Christmas is annually obscured by our commercialized, consumerist, materialistic, market driven culture. Madison Avenue type marketing continues to turn our attention away from the message of the coming of the Christ child to how we can get the best deals and the lowest prices on the latest gadgets and garments for our gifts.

It's so bad sometimes that even we Christians have to be reminded that Christmas is not about getting nice gifts from a fat man in a red suit; it's about a getting the greatest gift from a loving God with a big heart. Christmas is not really about expensive gifts wrapped in pretty paper and laid under a Christmas tree. It's about the greatest gift, a savior wrapped in swaddling clothes and lying a manger.

And while it is a blessing to have peaceful fellowship with family and friends, the greatest blessing is to have peace with God, which results in the peace of God, through his son our savior. Christmas is about the birth of Christ. He is still the reason for the season.

By the time of this text, Zechariah and Elizabeth have been told by the angel Gabriel that the savior is coming and that their child would be John the forerunner of Christ. An angel has already come to Mary to tell her that she would be the mother of the Messiah. An angel has also encouraged Joseph in a dream to take Mary as his wife, assuring him that the child in her womb is of God and is a "holy thing." Caesar has made his decree that the entire world be taxed, forcing Joseph and Mary to travel to Bethlehem, the city of their lineage, to register. While in Bethlehem, Mary has Jesus who is born in a barn in Bethlehem because there was no room for them in the Inn. The Magi, often referred to as the wise men, have seen the star and traveled to see the newborn babe. Once they arrive, they bow before him and offer him gifts fit for a king. But once they decide to leave, having been warned in a dream not to return to Herod, the text reports that "they leave another way."

Somewhere in the sequence of those events, our text records the announcement of the birth of Jesus given to an unlikely group in an unprecedented way. The group is some shepherds quietly keeping watch over their flocks by night. As a matter of fact they were just doing their job, minding their own business, when all of a sudden they were are interrupted by the appearance of an angel.

When you hear the word "interrupted," it usually carries with it negative connotations. The common attitude among people is that they rarely like to be interrupted when they are engaged in what they consider to be important. Usually when we are interrupted our initial response is to be upset and even irritable. But all interruptions are not bad. Some interruptions are an unexpected blessing.

And here in the text, these shepherds experience a pleasant interruption. Their initial response is one of fear. In fact the Bible says that they were "terrified." But the angel tells them 'fear not'. I bring you good news and great joy that will be for all the people. Today in the town of David a Savior has been born to you: he is Christ the Lord. This will be a sign to you: You will find a baby wrapped in cloths and lying in a manger" (Luke 2:10-12). Then the text says, "Suddenly a great company of the heavenly host appeared with the angel, praising God and saying, "Glory to God in the highest; And on earth peace to men on Whom his favor rests" (Luke 2:13-14).

What an announcement! From our vantage point in history this is clearly the most important news from heaven ever announced. The savior of the world has finally come, born in Bethlehem. And yet, God does not make a broad announcement to the entire world in one sweeping gesture. He does not take the pen of time, dip it in the ink of eternity and write the good news of his sons' birth on the backdrop of the nocturnal sky. But instead, when he first goes public, he chooses a few anonymous shepherds in an unknown field, keeping watch over their flocks by night. He does not choose to make the news known first to princes, potentates, the prestigious or the powerful. He doesn't even choose to announce the fulfillment of the prophecy of the coming king to the priests and religious leaders of the day.

Instead he chooses as his first full audience, shepherds watching sheep at night. Shepherds would have been considered outcasts in the minds of the average Orthodox Jew. After all, they could not keep the rituals necessary to maintain the ritual cleanliness while perpetually out watching sheep. Furthermore, their jobs kept them away from Temple attendance for extended periods of time. They should have been the last people chosen as custodians of such incredible news.

But that's just the way God is. God has a way of surprising us by choosing the most unlikely people to use and bless. Don't ever think that your station and stature in life exempts you from receiving revelation from the Lord and being used by the Lord in extraordinary ways. God trusted some common people with an uncommon message! They were just out in a field doing the ordinary. But right there in the midst of the ordinary, God does something extraordinary. God is often doing the extraordinary in the midst of the ordinary. He did it back then and he is still doing it now. They couldn't get to the temple but God met them in the field and blessed them right where they were. Don't make the mistake of confining the presence or move of God to the precincts of a sanctuary. God is speaking, moving and blessing in the midst of the ordinary.

Right there on your job, at your home, in your car, at your desk, on campus, in your apartment, wherever there is a "there" God can bless you. In the midst of the mundane, God is prepared to do the miraculous! God uses ordinary people, doing ordinary things, in ordinary places to do the extraordinary!!!!

The shepherds were the recipients of some astounding news. What was the news? This day, in the city of David, the savior is born! They heard the good news of the birth of the savior, an event so incredible that it split history into BC and AD. They were given a sign: "And this shall be a sign unto you; Ye shall find the babe wrapped in swaddling clothes, lying in a manger" (Luke 2:12). It is the angels' way of saying, "I know you want to go see him. And this is how you will find him." Then, out of nowhere a celestial choir shows up standing in mid air on an invisible platform of solidified molecules singing.

It was the custom of that culture and day that when a male child was born that the musicians would come to the place and sing songs to celebrate. But Jesus' birth went almost altogether unnoticed. There was no village celebration in song to accompany his birth. But what men didn't do, angels did. An angelic choir sang and praised, singing this song: "Glory to God in the highest, and on earth peace, good will toward men" (Luke 2:14). Notice that the praise declares first God, then the peace. You can't have true peace apart from God. The Pax Romana, or the peace of Rome was predicated upon the absence of war. There was peace in Rome because of the power of the Roman army to keep peace. But the absence of war is not the same thing as the presence of peace. The peace that comes from God is Shalom. That peace means wholeness, prosperity, soundness. God is the source of true peace. Peace with God leads to having the peace of God. And when you have the true peace of God, then you can live in true peace with others.

Once the angels departed after declaring the good news of the birth of Christ, the shepherds were not satisfied with just knowing that he was born, they went to see for themselves. It should never be enough for you to just hear about the savior. It is better to come to know the savior for yourself. The shepherds went to see for themselves. In fact, verse 16 says that they got in a hurry and went to find Mary and Joseph so that they could see the child for themselves. After seeing the baby for themselves, the very next verse (v. 17) reports that they spread the word about Jesus. That is the blessed privilege and responsibility of everyone who comes to know the Lord and Christ for themselves.

At the first Christmas, God used stars, shepherds, angels and magi to announce the birth of Christ, now God uses us! All who heard the good news of Christ from the lowly shepherds were amazed at what they heard (v.18). But there is a brief insertion in the text that reports that Mary pondered those things in her heart.

Here we have two wonderful responses to the news of the coming of the savior to the world. There was the amazement of some. And the news of the coming of the savior to the world is truly amazing news! It is one thing to know that there is a God above us. And it is also one thing to believe that this God above us is sufficient to meet our needs. But it is truly another thing to hear that the great God above us has come among us! He is Emmanuel, God with us! What an incredible truth. The love of God is so strong for us, that God personally came to see about us in Christ our Lord.

He is touched by all of our infirmities. That is what the scriptures report. When the Lord came to save us, in the process, he exposed himself to all of the things in life that touch our lives: the joys and pains, the celebrations and struggles, the triumphs and the temptation, the delights and the disappointments, the ups and downs, the good and the bad, the poverty, pain, the oppression, brutality, mistreatments, the hardships, heartache, hard times, hunger, hellish situations.

We serve a God who knows how we feel; who identifies with our life struggles because he came to our world to shiver in our cold and sweat in our heat. He does more than sympathize, he empathizes! He has been through what we have been through. The only difference is that he was able to carve out a way of triumph in the midst of tragedy. He was tempted by sin but knew no sin and he struggled against the harsh realities of life and won! "In this world" he said, "you will have tribulation, but be of good cheer, I have overcome the world (John 16:33)! The masses responded to the good news with amazement but what Jesus did for us is amazing.

The text also notes that Mary pondered those things in her heart. That's the other response to the news of the coming of the Lord. Mary did more than respond superficially to what she heard. She took them to heart and meditated on them. That is what we ought to do as well. It is not enough for us to be excited and amazed! That's just considering the good news of Jesus on the surface of things. We need to take the time to think deeply about the meaning of Jesus and his love in our lives! What does it mean to know Christ? What does it mean to be his disciples? What does it mean to receive his love? What does it mean to follow him? It's good to know that the love of God in Christ saves our souls, but ponder in your heart the implications of discipleship. Let the seed of the truth of the coming of Christ in your life take root deep in your heart today.

Finally the text says in verse 10 that the shepherds returned. Of course that phrase means that they returned to where they had come from. They returned to what they had been doing. But even though they returned to the same place, they did not return as the same men. They had been deeply affected by their encounter with Christ. My prayer is that once the celebration of the birth of Christ is over--once the season has ended, once the holidays are over, once all presents are opened and the gifts enjoyed, once our loved ones go back home and we go back to our families, our places of work and the routine of our daily responsibilities--we don't go back to the same thing the same way. For Christmas is more than gifts, eggnog, turkey, time off, relaxation, Christmas carols, and a good time. Christmas is about Christ. It's about a savior who came to deliver us from that which has separated us from our God and give us a chance to have a personal relationship with the Lord. And no one can truly have an encounter with Christ and go back to business as usual.

HOW TO HAVE GOOD SUCCESS

Joshua 1:1-8

1Now after the death of Moses the servant of the LORD it came to pass, that the LORD spake unto Joshua the son of Nun, Moses' minister, saying, 2Moses my servant is dead; now therefore arise, go over this Jordan, thou, and all this people, unto the land which I do give to them, even to the children of Israel. 3Every place that the sole of your foot shall tread upon, that have I given unto you, as I said unto Moses. 4From the wilderness and this Lebanon even unto the great river, the river Euphrates, all the land of the Hittites, and unto the great sea toward the going down of the sun, shall be your coast. 5There shall not any man be able to stand before thee all the days of thy life: as I was with Moses, so I will be with thee: I will not fail thee, nor forsake thee. 6Be strong and of a good courage: for unto this people shalt thou divide for an inheritance the land, which I sware unto their fathers to give them. 7Only be thou strong and very courageous, that thou mayest observe to do according to all the law, which Moses my servant commanded thee: turn not from it to the right hand or to the left, that thou mayest prosper withersoever thou goest. 8This book of the law shall not depart out of thy mouth; but thou shalt meditate therein day and night, that thou mayest observe to do according to all that is written therein: for then thou shalt make thy way prosperous, and then thou shalt have good success.

Everyone likes to succeed. In fact, I don't know anyone who likes to fail. To be sure, it is often true that one can learn more from one's failures than one's success. But the reason we want to learn from our failures is so that we can learn to succeed. In fact, we live in a society that is obsessed with the notion of success. Now granted, the world's images and ideas of success are often misguided, twisted and perverted but behind it all is still the ache for success, a desire to achieve. I believe this basic instinct is from God. The spirit within, when healthy, is never satisfied with business as usual. It can never really get used to mediocrity. It can never truly be comfortable with the status quo.

There is something in the human spirit that yearns to rise, to accomplish, to achieve and improve. We may resist this at times and sink back into comfort zones. Fear may cause us to bury the itch for success and ache for accomplishment deep within us. But as soon as we get around someone who is achieving, someone who is talking success talk, someone who seems determined to rise to a higher level in their lives, something stirs on the inside of us. Something vibrates. Something trembles. The soul begins to reach again. When the soul is healthy it reaches towards betterment. For instance, if you had a bad year last year, you want a good year this year. If you had a good year last year you want a better year this year. All of us want to succeed, to achieve something worthwhile, to move higher, to make something meaningful of our lives.

In our text, Joshua is about to lead the children of Israel across the Jordan River into the Promised Land, the land of their inheritance. They can literally look over and see what God has promised. As they prepare to cross over, God is giving Joshua some final instructions for crossing over into a land that they have never inhabited before. He is giving Joshua these instructions because he wants Joshua and the people to succeed in taking the land. You may be standing in a place, ready to cross over into a new land and God wants you to have success. In this passage we have a biblical formula for good success.

DEAD THINGS

The first thing the Lord says to Joshua before they cross over is to leave dead things behind. "Moses my servant is dead. Now then…cross the Jordan river into the land…" (v.1-2). God was trying to indicate that they should leave dead Moses behind. Now, that is not always easy to do. Some things we lose are very precious to us. Some of us lost jobs, relationships, material possessions, promising opportunities and even people that meant so much to us. It hurts to know that we cannot get them back. But the problem with some of us is that we are tempted to conclude that we cannot go on without them. However, that is a lie. In fact, when God told Joshua, "Moses is dead...now cross over..." he was essentially telling Joshua, "Listen. Moses is dead. I am not dead. And what you and Israel need in order to have good success in the land of promise is me, not Moses." God later reinforces this fact by promising Joshua, "As I was with Moses, so shall I be with you" (v.5).

I do not want to seem insensitive when I say, "leave dead things behind." I am not suggesting that you pretend like the loss does not hurt. Loss is painful. When losses happen, take time to mourn. It is all right to mourn. It is healthy to mourn over the dead. However, do not get stuck in that period of mourning. After you mourn, leave that dead thing behind and move on. It is interesting to note that God did indeed allow Joshua and the people time to mourn for Moses. But there was a time limit to the mourning. God gave them 30 days (Deut 34:8). By doing that God was saying, "You can pause but don't park. You can stop but don't stay. You can give your mourning a moment but not a lifetime." Mourn but move on. When Job lost people and things precious to him the Bible says he didn't simply put ashes on his head as a sign of mourning, but he went and sat down in the ashes (Job 2:8). Be careful not to sit down and stay in ashes. Do not camp out in your disappointment. Do not lounge in your loss. Do not park permanently in the pain. Perhaps you need to leave a dead relationship behind. I know you thought you would walk down the aisle with that person. I know you thought they would be Mr. Him or Mrs. Her. But it didn't work out. It died. Go ahead and cry but wipe your tears while you are walking forward. Perhaps you need to leave a lost marriage behind. That marriage you once had is over. The divorce is final. Your former spouse is remarried and has gone on with his or her lives. It is time for you to do the same. Quit hoping that someday you will be back together. It is dead.

Perhaps you need to leave the disappointment of a lost opportunity behind. Stop whining over that lost opportunity you missed. That opportunity is dead. It will never come again. But there are some new, exciting and living opportunities over in the promised land of future possibilities. But how are you ever going to meet them if you stay stuck at the gravesite of your last lost chance? Bury that thing and move forward! Maybe you need to leave the pain of what your enemies did to you behind. They were cruel and it was not right and you did not deserve what they did. Forgive your enemies. Be free of the dead weight of unforgiveness. Don't carry that dead body over the Jordan with you. Leave that dead body and cross over into good success.

God was serious about Joshua leaving dead Moses behind. In fact, God buried Moses. He would not let the people bury Moses. When God buried Moses he buried him in an undisclosed place (Deut. 34:6). He did that because he knew that those people were so attached to Moses that if they had buried him, right before they crossed over they would have dug him back up and dragged his dead carcass over the Jordan with them. Leave dead things behind. Let it, let them, let her or let him go!

There is just no getting around it. In order to move forward with God, you will just have to leave some things behind. The blind Bartimaeus left his cloak behind before he got his sight (Mark 10:50). Zacchaeus left the crowd behind before he could successfully see Jesus (Luke 19:2-4). The disciples left everything behind before they could successfully follow Jesus (Luke 18:28).

CLAIM YOUR INHERITANCE

The second thing we need to do in order to have good success is to claim our inheritance (v. 3-4). While there are some things behind us that God wants us to leave, there are some things ahead of us that God wants us to pursue. Leave what God does not want you to have but claim what God does want you to have. Now, in order for you to claim your inheritance, you have to have a vision of what it is that you have inherited. God gave Joshua the specific dimensions of the Promised Land. He did this to give Joshua and the people a vision of their inheritance. God will do the same for you as you move into new beginnings. God will give you a glimpse of your destiny. Discover God's vision for your life. Discover his purpose for you. That is your inheritance. Let God open your eyes to what he would have you become and what he wills for you to accomplish. He has a divine plan for you and he wants to reveal it to you by his Spirit.

After you catch a vision of your inheritance then claim your inheritance. That means that you must have faith. Claim it. Act as if it is yours already. Walk like it is yours. Talk like it is yours. You must first discover what is yours and then claim it because you cannot claim what is not yours. However, if God has it for you, it is yours. Claim it! Claim who God wants you to be. Claim where God wants you to go. Claim what God wants you to achieve. Claim what God wants you to have. Claim what God wants you to do. Claim what God is showing you. By faith, claim what God has bequeathed you.

GOD'S PROMISES

A third thing you need to do if you are going to have good success is to lean on God's promise (v.5). As with most times when you are stepping out on what God has promised you, there will be opposition. The enemy will not let you succeed unopposed. You will have to fight. But you have something exciting going for you. You've got a promise. Learn to lean on God's promises.

God promises Joshua, "There shall not be any man able to stand before thee..." (v.5). I believe that promise is true for us as well. What God is saying in substance is that when you pursue the things of God the enemy will not be able to stop you. Now, God doesn't say that the enemy will not try to stop you. The promise is that the enemy will not be able to stop you. The promise is not that no weapon will be formed against you. The promise is that no weapon will be able to prosper (Is. 54:17). You will have the victory. You will realize your inheritance.

GOOD SUCCESS IS CONDITIONAL

There are two additional things you need to do if you are going to have good success. If you take note of the boundaries of the Promised Land set by God in verse, you will see there is a difference between the boundaries that God set for the inheritance and the land that the people actually ended up having. They did not reach the full limit of their inheritance. God set out the boundaries of the inheritance that God intended for Joshua and the nation to acquire. However, they never reached the frontiers that God intended. They did not finish. They ended up with less. This is often the case with us. The design and plan God has for our life is so much greater than we realize. The question remains then, why is it that the children of Israel did not realize all the land that God promised? It is because receiving the full inheritance is conditional.

The first condition you must meet is that you must adopt the right attitude (v. 6-7). God said, "Be strong." This speaks of human effort and human effort is a necessary part of the equation of success. God says to Joshua in verse 3, "Every place that the sole of your foot shall tread upon, that have I given unto you, as I said unto Moses!" God has marked out the territory but they had to walk it out. They did not get all that was promised because they stopped short. The question for you is, how far can you walk?

How much territory can you cover? How much effort are you willing to put forth? When the text says, "Every place that the sole of your foot shall tread upon, that have I given unto you, as I said unto Moses," it means that you will have to pick up your foot, move it forward and then put it back down. That takes effort. Too many believers miss their inheritance because they want God to do all the work. Do not think that possessing your inheritance will roll in on the wheels of inevitability. God will not hand it to you on a silver platter. Claiming your inheritance is a heaven and earth, dust and divinity, you and God collaborative effort. God will do God's part; however, you have to do your part. If you want good grades in school, you can't just pray for them. You have to study for them. If you want a job, you can't just claim it by faith. You have to go out and look for it. If you want a promotion on your job, you can't just trust God. You have to put in some work. If you want money, you have to earn it. If you want godly children, you have to raise them in a godly manner. If you want a praying spirit, then you have to pray. If you want strong faith, then you have to exercise the faith you already have. God will do his part but he is encouraging you to do your part.

Your part is to put in the effort. You are to be strong as you do it. You are to do your part with all your might. You are to persist in your effort. Do not stop short of God's vision for you. You have to keep stepping until you realize all that God has shown you. It will not be easy. There are times it will be a fight and there are times that you will want to give up, stop short and settle for less. Do not do it. Do not quit. Instead, "be strong."

God also said, "be...of good courage." Do not be afraid. The scripture teaches us that, "God has not given us a spirit of fear, but of power, love and of a sound mind" (2 Tim. 1:7). In other words, have faith. Faith requires fearlessness. It requires risk taking. It requires leaving the comfort zone. It requires engaging the enemy. It requires moving at God's command without hesitation. When you are moving towards your inheritance, there are times when faith demands that you act as if you have nothing to lose and live like nothing can stop you. You have to let faith emancipate you from fear. Fear is the enemy of good success. Face future tasks knowing that, "all things are possible to him that believes" (Mark 9:23).

The second condition you must meet if you are going to realize the promise of good success is to make sure that whatever you do, you do it by the book (v.8). What you pursue is important however, how you pursue it is just as important. If you are going to have good success then you must pursue it making sure that you live in obedience to the Word of God. You have to do it God's way. God's word teaches God's way. The children of Israel failed to reach the full frontiers that God designed because they did not meet the divine requirements of doing it God's way. You cannot ignore God's way and have good success. You cannot do things your own way and have good success. The Word declares that, "there is a way that seemeth right unto man, but the end thereof are the ways of death" (Prov. 16:25). You have to do it by the book. If you do, Psalms 1, verse 3, says you "shall be like a tree planted by the rivers of water that brings forth fruit in its season, its leaves shall not wither and whatsoever he doeth shall prosper." When you do it God's way, you will have good success.

Finally, please note that the scriptures do not simply speak of success, they speak of good success. The very fact that the text says good success suggests that is possible to have bad success. One definition of success is when you set a goal you reach it. That is the kind of success the world teaches. Set a goal and if you reach that goal you have succeeded. If your goal is to be a rich businessman and if you are a businessman and become rich, then you are a success. If your goal is to be a popular preacher, then as you soon as you are a preacher you become popular, then you are a success. Now, that sounds fine. However there is a flaw in that brand of success. You say you are a successful businessman because you reached your goal of becoming rich. But suppose you became rich by resorting to underhanded and unethical business practices? Is that good success? You say you are a successful preacher because you are popular and you are in great demand as a speaker. But suppose you became a popular speaker by compromising the truth and majoring in telling people what they want to hear instead of what they need to hear? Is that good success?

Good success is not setting a goal and reaching it. Good success is when you find your purpose and fulfill it. That is good success. For example, John Hastings wrote in The Speakers Bible Commentary, that the purpose of a clock is to tell time. As long as it is fulfilling the purpose for which it was created it is a success. However, if it ceases to accurately tell time then no matter how beautiful a mantelpiece it makes, it is not a success. It is not fulfilling its purpose. An axe head is created to cut wood. You can use it as a paperweight and it may hold the paper down. But it is not a success until it cuts wood, because that is what it is created for.[2]

You are created for a purpose. You are created to glorify God. As long as your life glorifies God then you are having good success. How do you glorify God? Find out your particular purpose and fulfill it. God has a purpose for your life. Talk to God about your purpose. Seek to fulfill His particular purpose for your life and as you fulfill it, that will be good success.

This definition of success is why Jesus was successful. He was in no way a success by earthly standards but he was by heaven's standards. He was not a success because he was rich, because he wasn't. The Bible says, "He became poor…" (2 Cor. 8:9). He was not a success because he owned real estate because he didn't. He declared, "Foxes have holes and birds of the air have nests but the

---

[2] Hasting, James The Speakers Bible Commentary (The Books of Deuteronomy, Joshua, Judges and Ruth 2. Grand Rapids Michigan: Baker Book House, 1087) 212

son of man has nowhere to lay his head" (Luke 9:58). He was not a success because he was published, because he wasn't. He never had a book bound or a best seller. He was not a success because he was well traveled. I understand he never traveled more than a few hundred miles from his hometown. He was not a success because he was popular. They crucified him on a criminal's cross. No, he was not a success by the world's standards but he was a success. He was a success because he discovered and fulfilled his purpose. He discovered and did the Father's will. He was a success because one day he declared, "I must be about my Father's business?" (Luke 2:49). He was a success because he said his greatest fulfillment was, "to do the will of him who sent me" (John 4:34). He was a success because he did what the Father told him to do and said what the Father told him to say. He was a success because he died on Calvary and dying on Calvary was his purpose. He came to die. He declared, "For this cause came I...." (John 12:27). He lives to show us how to live. Then he died that we might have a right to live. Then he got up early on a Sunday morning so that we can live forever more. I am so glad that Jesus had good success. He found his purpose and fulfilled it. And because he found and fulfilled his, you can find and fulfill your dream!

About the Author

Dr. F. Bruce Williams was born July 19, 1959 to Rev. Earl B. and Norrene T. Williams at Langley Air Force Base in Hampton, Virginia. Early in life, God ordained Dr. Williams' footsteps.

Earning numerous honors, he graduated Summe Cum Laude from Florida A & M University and went on to obtain his Masters of Divinity from Southern Baptist Theological Seminary and his Doctorate in Ministry from the United Theological Seminary.

Dr. Williams was installed as Senior Pastor of Bates Memorial Baptist Church, located in Smoketown, one of the poorest zip codes in Jefferson County, Louisville, Kentucky, in 1986 after serving as an associate minister. Twenty-five years later, the congregation has grown exponentially, seeing its membership increase from a hundred members to over five thousand members.

Dr. Williams is committed to changing the lives of the marginalized, people that society has forgotten. The homeless, the drug addicts, the single mothers, the hurting and the suffering all have a purpose and a place in the Kingdom. Through his message of transformation and restoration, Dr. Williams encourages people to believe God, to believe in themselves, and to believe that there is something greater for their lives. He desires that all people seek after and discover their God-ordained purpose by introducing them to the power of the Savior.

Dr. Williams is married to the former Leona Michelle Smith of Greensboro, Florida. Dr. F. Bruce and Dr. Michelle Williams are the proud parents of two daughters, Imani Colette and Nailah Cymone.

ALSO AVAILABLE BY DR. WILLIAMS:

GIDEON- A HERO IN THE MAKING

Frightened, defeated, oppressed and suffering from a severe case of poor self esteem, Gideon was the most unlikely answer to his nation's need for a liberator and leader. But God has a way of choosing the most unlikely people to rise to greatness and even alter the course of history.

A Hero in the Making is a series of sermons that charts how God carefully, skillfully, patiently and miraculously makes and molds a man named Gideon into the hero that God intended for him to be and into the hero his nation sorely needed. God literally transforms the life of one of the "least of these" and uses him to deliver a nation.

However, this book is not just a story of what God did in the life of Gideon; it's a lesson in what God can do in your life too! No matter where people, circumstances, hardships or even personal mistakes have put you, God is not finished with you yet! You may not see it, and others may not see it, but God sees within you the stuff of which heroes are made. And if you would trust God with your life, God will take who you are - past, present and future - and begin to mold and make you with his cosmically capable hands and you, too, can become a hero in the making!

Contact Information

www.fbrucewilliamsministries.com

fbw@fbrucewilliamsministries.com

Bates Memorial Baptist Church

620 E. Lampton Street

Louisville, KY 40203

Made in the USA
Columbia, SC
15 March 2019